1173

Industry and Values

INDUSTRY AND VALUES

The Objectives and Responsibilities of Business

edited by

Michael Ivens

*Director, the Industrial Educational
and Research Foundation*

with a Foreword by

Sir John Reiss

*Chairman of the Trustees, the Industrial Educational
and Research Foundation*

George G. Harrap & Co. Ltd
London   Toronto   Wellington   Sydney

First published in Great Britain 1970
by GEORGE G. HARRAP & Co. LTD
182 High Holborn, London, W.C.1

© *Industrial Educational and*
Research Foundation 1970

SBN 245 59891 X

Composed in Old Style type and printed at
the Pitman Press, Bath
Made in Great Britain

Foreword

by SIR JOHN REISS

(Chairman of the Trustees of the Industrial
Educational and Research Foundation)

This book deals with a subject that has not been systematically explored—that of the values and ethical standards of industry. This does not mean, of course, that businessmen operate in a moral vacuum. They share the values of their fellow-countrymen, but they make their choices and construct their principles in relation to different circumstances.

Profitability is a basic yardstick of the success of business operations, but it is not the only one. In practice the businessman has a wide variety of responsibilities to balance. His problems may include his responsibilities to the community, to what extent he should co-operate with the Government, the needs of his employees, customers, suppliers, and the trade unions. Finally, as many hard-pressed businessmen discover, there are his responsibilities to his family and also to himself: to what extent does he allow the pressure of business to dull some of his spiritual and intellectual ambitions?

The Industrial Educational and Research Foundation is concerned with the objectives and responsibilities of business, and *Industry and Values* makes a useful contribution to this field. Its contributors include a number of men who have given valuable assistance to the Foundation in its work.

Other organizations have also been doing interesting work in this field, notably St George's House, Windsor. Others include Political and Economic Planning, the British Institute of Management, and the William Temple College.

Industry and Values contains a number of different viewpoints. This reflects industry, which is very much a pluralistic society, with people of differing religions and others who are not committed in any way.

Nevertheless many decisions do have ethical and social implications, and this entails hard thinking and sometimes hard feeling.

The values of management and those of other groups do not always completely coincide, and here, as Dr Zweig has indicated, some communication 'bridges' need to be built.

Finally, industry needs to be intellectually coherent about its objectives as well as efficient in achieving them. *Industry and Values* will have made a useful contribution if it helps those of us in business to think about and clarify our objectives.

Preface

Industry and Values represents widely differing viewpoints and experiences. Contributors include businessmen, theologians, economists, directors of major industrial organizations, sociologists, academics, writers, and consultants.

The book does, I think, break some new ground, although inevitably it leaves some aspects untouched. The philosopher and the semanticist would, no doubt, have useful comments to make on some of industry's language of values.

Some of the contributors write from a Christian viewpoint, others are agnostic or uncommitted. All have been extraordinarily helpful in tackling some of the intractable business problems of our time: industry's relations with Government, the conflicting values of management and other groups, industry's varying responsibilities to shareholders, employees, customers, the community, the trade unions, and so on.

Many of the writers have, in addition, tackled these problems in their own work and lives, and this does, I think, lend the contributions additional interest and authority. The subject of organizations and values is, in fact, a practical one, and decisions are inescapable. Sometimes it can lead to conflict, as in Edward Holloway's actual case study.

We are grateful to all contributors for their help and patience. Also to the European Association for Personnel Management for permission to reproduce Professor Solomon Barkin's paper on "The Social Setting for Modern Personnel Management", which was first delivered at a conference in Stockholm, and *British Industry* for permission to use material from "In Search of a Business Philosophy", on which the Introduction has been based.

MICHAEL IVENS

Contents

Introduction

by MICHAEL IVENS

Michael Ivens is Director of the Industrial Educational and Research Foundation. He is the author and editor of a number of books on industry: *The Practice of Industrial Communication, Case Studies in Management; Case Studies in Human Relations, Productivity and Organization; Case Studies in Marketing, Finance and Control;* and *The Case for Capitalism.* He is joint editor of *Twentieth Century Magazine,* political adviser to the Junior Hospital Doctors' Association, and the author of two books of poetry. He set up the first industrial communication organization in this country for Esso Petroleum.

One of the most significant changes in British industry during the past twenty years has been the wholesale acceptance of management-training. Starting as a trickle after the war— the occasional homage to Harvard and the importation of TWI courses—it has grown to a flood, both of activity and money.

The creation of efficient managers is a worth-while object. And yet, as one surveys the political, social, and cultural climate of Britain, one cannot help feeling that this has been a rather lop-sided development.

Some of the most important questions facing us concern the future role of private industry, the principles that should underlie its functions, its relationship with the Government, the community, its shareholders, workers, trade unions, and customers. Especially today, industry cannot operate in a conceptual or moral vacuum. Government is more and more impinging on it and involving it in important, qualitative choices and decisions. The inevitability of capitalism and of the entrepreneur are being questioned by men whose opinions are influential.

These questions cannot be deferred until our managers are efficient. Nor can they be considered in isolation from the role

11

and the responsibilities of the director. His answers to these questions will determine the objectives of the company and, thus, the decisions of his management.

This lop-sidedness, which has led to a glut of management-training and not sufficient attention being given to actual principles underlying business decisions and the changing responsibilities of boards of directors, arises partly because of a fallacy. That fallacy is the theory of the manager as a pure *decision-maker*.

The most solid defence of this theory was put forward by Eichmann during his trial in Jerusalem. His job, he argued, was to process Jews through concentration camps. He was just a manager. The objectives were not his business. The court, not unsurprisingly, rejected this theory of the manager as the pure decision-maker.

Nor can we import the Eichmann concept of management into industry. In practice there is an interaction between directors and managers regarding the objectives of the organization. Boards may take their decisions on social and ethical grounds as well as in relation to their responsibilities to the shareholder, the need for profit and to maintain the business. But the *qualitative* as well as the *quantitative* reasons for the decisions will almost certainly be communicated to, and discussed with, management.

The big difficulty, of course, is not just to determine the principles governing business activities but to see how these principles should be interpreted in practice. This was brought out quite strikingly, for example, in some of the speeches at a recent Institute of Directors' Annual Conference.

Sir Paul Chambers raised the question as to whether directors should co-operate with Government measures which they believed to be basically wrong, or whether they should as individuals or organizations refuse. "On balance I think not," commented Sir Paul. "Where we feel some good might be done by co-operation I believe it is our duty to co-operate, however disappointed or disillusioned some of us may be."

This is certainly clear. But it does raise some interesting questions. What if a director does not feel that 'some good' might be done? What then? And how shall we define 'good'—in terms of the country, company, shareholder, and employee? And what weight shall we give these factors?

Sir Paul was also explicit when it came to Government policy resulting in the centralization of decisions and the curtailment of liberties of individuals, companies, and trade unions. These were "bad both morally and as a matter of economic policy" and should be resisted.

Cardinal Heenan, however, landed us with thornier problems. "You can no longer say 'business is business' to justify sharp practice," and who would disagree with him? "Social justice—not profit—must be the first motive," however, is more arguable. "Social justice" as defined by whom? And can we put it before profit and efficiency—or should it not be an accompanying principle?

Mr Quintin Hogg's contribution was also related to this subject. Political freedom and economic freedom were related. This should be preached by management. So should the importance of risk-bearing and innovation.

The director, then (if one accepts Mr Hogg's point of view), must see the relation between his activities and political freedom, and state them openly.

I have cited these remarks from Sir Paul Chambers, Archbishop Heenan, and Mr Quintin Hogg, not just because they are interesting and important, but because they do contrast with the view that the director's job is merely to obey the law and to maximize profits for his shareholders (though Dr Alex Rubner, in particular, has argued that too much is ploughed back and not enough handed out to the shareholders—who ought to have the responsibility for reinvesting it).

American Thinking

This is very much in accord with some influential American thinking. In *The American Creed* (Harvard, 1956) F. X. Sutton and his colleagues stated that most leading American concerns had made the transition from 'classical' to 'managerial' objectives. They gave a high priority to profit and the shareholders' interests, but not an exclusive one. Other interests— such as those of customers, employees, suppliers, distributors, local communities, and the national community in terms of price policy, defence, and regional development—also had to be taken into account. But, as Professor Fogarty[1] put it in his excellent PEP study, *Wider Business Objectives*, "the priority given to these interests remained obscure. Some firms were more bound by market or political or social pressures than others, but nearly all had some freedom of manoeuvre."

The need, then, is to clarify the principles and to work out criteria. This has led to a good deal of activity by American business and educationists—not all of it productive. In 1961, for example, the United States Department of Commerce sponsored the formation of a Business Ethics Advisory Council of businessmen and academics to define and raise the ethical standards of American business. The Council surveyed in 1962–63 the teaching on business ethics in about a hundred business schools. Not more than ten, it concluded, were doing a competent job in this field.

Extramural Activities

The National Industrial Conference Board has found it necessary to set up a Public Affairs Division, and estimated that chief executives of American corporations spent at least 40 per cent of their time in "dealing with environmental problems of governmental, civic, and community relations; philanthropy; and education generally" (NCB report for 1964). Five hundred companies, it added, had set up public-affairs programmes, and the number was growing steadily.

Educational approaches have included the tough, pragmatic slant of Harvard's course on "Planning in the Business Environment" and the Carnegie Institute of Technology's more philosophic approach in their course on "Ideas and the Changing Environment".

After the first flush of 'ethical' courses the word 'ethics' has grown less popular in the United States, and (as indicated by the Harvard and Carnegie courses) other phrases have been substituted.

These approaches have not been without their critics. The most influential has probably been Theodore Leavitt, who has argued that American business leaders have been paying much too much attention to their alleged responsibility to society, their employees, and so on. What they needed to do was to be efficient, make profits—and the problem would take care of itself.

To which one might add—well, at least the director needs to look at the evidence in order to arrive at the extreme Leavitt position. If one is to hold the doctrine of simple profit maximization, then one had better do so with intellectual rigour than merely blindly.

In Britain we have had, on the one hand, the *News Chronicle* case, in which the judgment re-emphasized quite clearly the responsibility of the company towards its shareholders and, on the other, an increasing volume of voices calling for firms to accept new responsibilities.

In my own opinion there is unlikely to be any potted philosophy of social responsibility that can be imported ready-made into boardrooms. Nor is it desirable to attempt to set up ethical formulae to deal with industrial situations as a whole.

Determining Principles

The first step is to examine some of the concepts, principles, and responsibilities that underlie business decisions. There are plenty to hand: the allocation of profit, the concept of ownership (important in view of the present fashion for co-determination), the rights of employees, relations between Government and industry, the role of trade unions, exports and profitability, definitions of monopoly, relations between companies and shareholders, and so on.

The second is to determine at what level and in what form directors or managers can be assisted in examining problems of this kind. Should it be at board level? Or should certain management-training include sessions dealing with these subjects in order to prepare men for complex board decisions involving economic, social, ethical, and political factors?

The Industrial Educational and Research Foundation was set up recently to work on these problems. As well as carrying out original studies it will also provide educational material to those working in management education. It has at present commissioned a study on what is being done in Britain in this field.

PEP is engaged in a study to examine how British boards do in fact balance all the various claims on their resources. PEP is also reviewing current thinking in Britain, Europe, and the United States on the future of companies and corporations.

The European Association of Management Training Centres has a project in hand on European business ethics. In Ireland,

Spain, and Holland there is research going on not dissimilar to that of PEP.

These individual approaches reflect the need of the times. There is a growing willingness by business to examine and accept its social responsibilities. At the same time the intellectual forces opposing private industry make it more and more necessary for the individual director to think through the full implications of business decisions and to achieve a coherent business philosophy. That philosophy will vary from one businessman to another, although a rigorous examination should help to produce some kind of common approach to many issues.

[1] Professor Michael Fogarty, *Wider Business Objectives; American Thinking and Experience* (PEP, 1966).

I | *Industry and Society*

by H. F. R. CATHERWOOD

H. F. R. Catherwood is Director-General of Britain's National Economic Development Council. The Council, which is representative of Government, management, and trade unions, plays an important part in formulating and implementing plans for national economic development over a period of years ahead and, through its industry committees, in developing industrial efficiency and productivity. Mr Catherwood, born in 1925, was the Managing Director of the British Aluminium Company, Ltd, before joining the Department of Economic Affairs as Chief Industrial Adviser in October 1964. An Ulsterman, he qualified as a chartered accountant in 1951 after reading history and law at Cambridge. He spent six years with Richard Costain, Ltd, international construction engineers, and was appointed Chief Executive after a year's service at the age of thirty. Mr Catherwood has been a member of the NEDC as Chief Industrial Adviser. He is a member of the British National Export Council. He is married with three children.

I remember during the war travelling in a workman's train somewhere between Stafford and Rugby and listening in my schoolboy innocence to a workman's description of the kind of lurid social life he imagined was led by the directors of the large electrical company for whom he and the rest of the carriage worked. Wine, women, and week-ends at Brighton were clearly their driving force, and the rest of the carriage didn't know whether to believe him or laugh at him. A few years later, when I was at Cambridge, one of the Fellows was talking about the directors of the same company. His brother was a master at a famous public school in the town where the company had their works, and he saw society in that small town as sharply distinguished between the poor but intellectually interesting members of the school staff and the wealthy, solid, but dull directors of this large industrial company. When I went from Cambridge to the City of London and met the bowler-hatted gentlemen on the commuter trains they seemed equally out of touch both with the realities of life on the shop floor and with the intellectual life of the university.

Twenty years later I still find these two great gulfs, one between the intellectual leaders of society and the industry which sustains this country, and the other within industry between directors and workers. There are still far too great gaps in human understanding and respect, and the bridging of these gaps must be a first priority in our society.

The majority of people in Britain today work in industry, and if industry and those responsible for its leadership are going to build bridges between themselves and society, then they had better begin with the gap in understanding in their own companies. Charity begins at home.

I am often struck when I go round a plant by the way in which a manager will tell you in great detail what the machine is doing but ignore completely the man working on it. Yet, when you do talk to the operator, he is most enlightening, and, incidentally, will tell you what really happens as opposed to what is supposed to happen—what is more, the interest which other people take in his work makes his job more meaningful and worthwhile. Top management can't spend all their time remembering the names of the hundreds of people who work in a plant, especially when there is, as so often, a high rate of labour turnover. But there is all the difference in the world between a management which is genuinely interested in the views of those who operate the plant and the management which simply regards them as part of the technical process. For every Frank Taylor prepared to go down to the site and argue with strikers there must be many more bowler-and-brolley managers who never pass the time of day with a shop steward from one year's end to another.

But it is not enough to take notice. A good manager must be prepared to listen. It is quite extraordinary how few people in life will really listen. Most people are much more anxious to put over their own view, and this applies to management as much as anyone else. The other day I was asked to see a very important person, and was sent in advance a whole list of the questions he wanted to ask. He was due to stay for half an hour. At the end of fifteen minutes he hadn't stopped talking, and just out of interest I thought I would wait until he asked me positively for my own views. He never did. At the end of half an hour I saw him out, and he was still talking! He was by no means unique. Listening is not easy, and listening to someone who is inarticulate is even harder. It requires a real sympathy and some understanding of his point of view. A shop steward of a large motor-car company once wrote a letter to *The Times* in which he said that it was wrong to suppose that management did not get their case over to the men. He said the management's case came across loud and clear. The real difficulty lay in getting the men's case back to the management. If the management really wanted to know what the men thought, then they should not rely on formal channels of consultation at times of crisis. They should have well-developed and continuous lines of communication with the real opinions of the men on the shop floor. The grapevine is better than nothing, but it is dangerous to rely on the grapevine. Open and continuous relations on a wide front are much better.

Nor is it enough simply to listen. One of the difficulties arising from the gulf in society is that people will not believe that other people really do have a different point of view. You can have the best and smoothest method of consultation possible and still have the most terrible misunderstandings. The men on the two sides of the table can be patient, amenable, and reasonable, and yet, because they have not seen inside each other's presuppositions, they can come to blows in the end. Communication is not just the art of putting over your point of view. It is also the art of getting inside the other man's skin. A management can get very wound up about the inability of the workers to see the need to keep costs down in order to remain competitive. But most workers do not have the same kind of stake in the company as the management, and they certainly do not have the same stake in the company as the shareholders. Of course, there are long-service employees with an emotional loyalty to the company. Of course, there are isolated towns where the whole work force depends on the prosperity of one company. But generally in Britain there is a large variety of work available and a fairly high degree of labour turnover. The weekly paid or hourly paid worker expects to get the current rate for the job regardless of the ability of a particular company to pay. He is not heavily involved in the fortunes of the company for which he is temporarily working, and long lectures to him based on the management's preoccupation with the future of the company are not really going to move him. That is the job of the company's management, and if they can't do it he will find a company with a management which can.

A friend of mine recently went to adjudicate in a wages dispute. The management assured him that the whole problem was psychological. The men were entirely unreasonable, they were in a moody frame of mind, and nothing management did or said seemed to make the slightest difference. My friend went down to the shop floor, talked to the men, looked at their wages system and at the details of the dispute. Within a day it was quite clear to him that the trouble was entirely practical and not at all psychological. The company had managed to build up the most appallingly jumbled and confused tangle of piecework rates he had ever seen. It was almost impossible for the men to relate their earnings at the end of the week to what they had done, and the whole system was calculated to produce the maximum of friction and misunderstanding. Had the top management been prepared to spend just a bit of time looking at it from the men's point of view, had they put themselves into the shoes of the working-man and tried to figure out the calculations themselves, no trouble would ever have arisen. It is the duty of management to bridge the gulf and to try to see the plant and the work through the eye of the worker.

Another and perhaps the most important duty of management is to respect the personality and dignity of the fellow human beings who work for them. I am not at all in favour of a return to paternalism. The attitude of the squire to the rustics, beneficent though it may have been in parts, was altogether too arrogant. Yet if society has changed from the master-and-servant relationship to a relationship of contract between employer and employee, the employer is still not released from the duty of care to those to whom he has given a contract of employment. The Factories Acts and similar legislation now ensure a minimum standard of physical care at the place of work. But many companies have rightly gone far beyond these minimum obligations. I am sure that it has done few of them any harm. It has always seemed to me that there is a stong correlation between a company's treatment of its employees and its profitability. The companies with good canteens, recreation grounds, welfare services, efficient first-aid rooms, regular medical check-ups, stringent safety regulations, and well-lit, clean, warm, and brightly painted working areas usually seem to be the ones which turn in the best record on the Stock Exchange. Some people may feel that mown grass and flowering shrubs around the tool-room are wasted on the characters within. I think they are wrong. I believe the people appreciate good working conditions and that a good environment creates good work. If management is careless about the conditions and surroundings the worker will most likely be careless about the work.

A good management is not just interested in welfare. It has to produce an effective enterprise, and to do this it has got to impose a degree of discipline. There is no purpose in discipline for the sake of discipline. But discipline is necessary for the benefit of the enterprise as a whole, and a good management will exercise control for the benefit of the majority. A slack enterprise benefits no one. An obvious need for discipline is in safety. Safety precautions do not happen. They require a hard and determined management. I remember hearing of a plant in Ireland which had two safety devices on a machine, neither of which could be unlocked without stopping the machine by going over to a wall switch twelve feet away. One operative, nevertheless, managed to kill himself by turning the wall switch with a twelve-foot rod and opening both safety devices while the machine was still running. And that management thought itself safety-conscious and determined! Most plants have dangerous machinery, and most people quickly get accustomed to the danger. The only really safe plant is one which not only has proper fencing, warning notices, moving parts coloured in red, and so on, but one where the new employee does not feel a fool when he obeys the safety instructions, because everyone seems to obey instinctively.

Discipline also extends to the supervision of work. I know one plant where the first-line supervision would not wear white coats as instructed because they didn't want to be seen to be the man who had to give the orders. They were then made to wear their white coats, but fifteen minutes after clocking-in time and fifteen minutes before clocking-out time there was not a white coat to be seen in the plant. They were all on tremendously-important work in some obscure corner where they couldn't see the late coming and early going. This plant was commonly known as "Butlins by the gas-works". But when a tougher management insisted that the orders were going to go out that night and that no-one was going home until they were packed and dispatched, the whole place took on a new lease of life. Very few people really enjoy fooling their lives away.

Management is interested in improving performance and cutting costs. Hours will be spent with the stop-watch and bar chart to perfect a method improvement. Hundreds of thousands of pounds will be spent on new machinery, and today this can run into thousands of pounds per man employed. But very seldom in these equations does job satisfaction emerge as major factor. We have all laughed at Charlie Chaplin's *Modern Times*, but many a job today is as devoid of any human interest. It is small wonder that work seems less important to most people than the winner of the 2.30 at Kempton Park. It is perfectly true that many men and perhaps more women get a kind of satisfaction from a routine job where once they have got into the rhythm they can think and talk about something quite different. Yet experiments have shown that if semi-skilled labour is left with an element of judgment in the job, if it is given something to watch out for, some choice to make, then performance will in fact be higher and not lower. Management, in my view, owes it to the worker to make his job interesting and to build a measure of job satisfaction into the working method. This is not cybernetics, it is just plain sense.

Perhaps the most important quality which a worker looks for in management is that it should be trustworthy. Precisely the same offer can be made by two different managements in exactly the same material circumstances. The one can be welcomed by the men, and the other can rightly be rejected. In the one case the men will take it that the offer is in good faith, and in the other they will, through hard and bitter experience, mistrust the meaning and motives of management. No-one minds a management which bargains hard. That is only to be expected. No-one even minds a management which points out forcibly the effects of failure to agree. But men resent dishonest threats, resent promises which imply more than is intended; they resent undertakings which are not kept. Trust takes years to build up. Once established it can be of invaluable benefit. At a crisis in the fortunes of a company the ability of men to believe the management can make all the difference between salvation and disaster. All misrepresentation is a form of contempt, and trust, which is long-lasting and endurable, can only come because men and management have a really deep and lasting respect for each other.

I have put the duties of management to worker first because today we do not hear enough about them. What we are told today on all sides is the duty of the worker to management and to society. There is much talk of revoking the legal protection which the employee has held for most of this century. People say that wildcats must be taken to law and sued and put in prison if they do not pay their fines. I believe that most of this is both unrealistic and wrong. But one does not have to hold these extreme views to believe that there is an obligation which the industrial worker has to the society in which he lives. The special position of trade-union activity under the law was created to protect the bargaining position of those whose only protection against society was their right to bargain collectively. Those who selfishly exploit a dearly bought privilege for the sake of small and impermanent gains run the risk of losing all that their fathers and grandfathers fought for. My personal view is that society would be most ill advised to try to revoke the legal protection of trade unions. But the workers' best protection against such ill-considered action is that they should behave responsibly.

Perhaps the most difficult problems of all are the practices which have traditionally been used to protect the worker but which have now ceased to have any useful purpose and are, instead, a positive hindrance both to full employment and to the advance in real wages. Most of the craft unions have restriction on intake. As a professional chartered accountant I cannot fault this in principle. My institute demands apprenticeship, and so do many of the craft unions. But the difficulty with all such bodies, my own included, is that times change, and the skills which society needs change with them. Both the craft unions and the professional societies have traditionally regarded it as their duty to enforce minimum standards for the exercise of their skills. But these skills must be continuously related to the needs of society and to the numbers of skilled people required if the economy of the nation is to go ahead. When the Regional Employment Premium was being discussed many industrialists said that the main reason why they did not go to development areas was not shortage of cash but the lack of skilled labour in the regions. Some time later I asked one of the men responsible for the Government training centres in one of the regions whether they were anywhere nearer relieving these shortages. He said his training centres were full but that union restrictions in his area meant that many of the people he had trained were finding jobs in Birmingham and London. In this case the inflexibility of some of the craft unions in maintaining their traditional restrictions of the use of retrained labour was not only ceasing to help them but, because the craft-based industries were in decline and they needed the new businesses in the region, it was also putting their own employment at risk.

Other restrictions arise out of nothing but pure selfishness. A large company in Manchester ordered a piece of equipment urgently from a firm in Widnes. The lorry-driver made a special journey and arrived over half an hour before the end of the shift. The foreman refused delivery. "The lads won't unload it," he said. "But my boss said you needed it urgently tonight." "I can't help that," said the foreman; "the lads like to get off pretty sharp, and they won't unload it now." The lorry-driver insisted that a near-by crane could lift off the single piece of equipment in two minutes and transfer it to the appropriate department the following day. This was refused, so he took the precaution of getting his arrival time signed at the gate, worried that his boss would think he had lingered over an urgent journey and had arrived too late. Next day, because the equipment had not been delivered and another journey was required, his boss was under fire from the Manchester plant, and so was he. Then he told the story, produced his driver's log, and the foreman was dismissed. The story was told to a friend of mine by the lorry-driver, a keen trade unionist, who felt that this kind of conduct was undermining all he had ever cared for and fought for.

Perhaps the greatest worry of the responsible trade unionist is the irresponsible trouble-maker. It is wrong, of course, to lay all the blame for trouble-makers on the unions. Trouble-makers get their best chance when there is trouble. A good management sees that there is as little trouble as possible. But an irresponsible trouble-maker also needs irresponsible men   the floor, men who are not prepared to think, not prepared to turn out and vote in their union elections, men who let their emotions run away with their judgment, men who are afraid to stand out for what they think right, or men who are prepared to follow someone just because he amuses them. Of course, there are times when the union is too remote and too overstretched to help the men in a particular shop. Someone takes the time and trouble to make their case to management and to bring pressure on both management and union. He may be a trouble-maker. But he may be a good man, doing a job that no-one else was prepared to do. The real mischief-maker is out to create and exploit misunderstanding. Any management must be thankful for a labour force than can see through this kind of man before he does any damage, and the longer men take to see through him, the more damage he can do to the company and to the community.

So large and complex is industry today and so recent in time are industrial organizations that the obligations of managements to managers are still a great uncharted sea. This subject is colloquially known as the 'rat-race' or 'power game', and is conducted by the shadowy figure of 'the organization man' or 'the man in the grey flannel suit'. Managers can have two kinds of relationship with the enterprise. They can have a purely market relationship, selling themselves to the highest bidder without any greater obligation than to do what they are paid to do. Or they can have a professional relationship, giving their full professional duty of care in return for a generally accepted level of professional reward. I believe that, so far as he can, the manager should act as a professional man and should give his services as unstintingly as a surgeon, a public servant, a judge, or an officer in the armed forces. There is a level of public responsibility at which it ill becomes a man to exploit a situation for the maximum personal gain. Yet a manager does not have the financial security of a judge or a public servant. His only security is his reputation. Ernest Marples said not long ago that he was asked to take over a company in difficulties and put it right. He felt that for a person who depended on his professional reputation the risk was too high. If he succeeded he would receive no reward but would keep his reputation. But if he failed, possibly through no fault of his own but simply because the company was beyond repair, his professional reputation and his future earning power would be damaged. In short, it was heads you lose and tails you don't win. High taxation made it impossible for him to obtain a premium which could cover the financial risk to his future earnings, and so he turned the job down. The manager, unlike the judge, is meant to take entrepreneurial risks. But if his risk premium is sliced down to nothing by progressive taxation, then the correct entrepreneurial decision is not to take the risk. Government is continually exhorting directors to take entrepreneurial risks, to export more or to invest more. They cannot understand their reluctance to take these risks. Indeed, only those who have stepped across the boundary between management and the public service realize the great gulf between the insecurity of one and the security of the other. I do not feel, therefore, that we should condemn too harshly the manager who sells his service to the highest bidder in an endeavour to achieve peak earnings while the going is good, who wants this security against the day when his earning power is seriously diminished or may be lost altogether through no fault of his own. Such anxiety about the future may produce hollow laughter from those whose earnings and perks are nowhere near as high as the earnings and perks of the bosses of British industry. In the days of the golden handshake and generous stock options the hollow laughter was perhaps justified. There are men who have made a fortune by being dismissed three times in quick succession. But the days of the stock option are over, the golden handshake has been cut down to size, and there is many a good manager who never came within sight of one or the other. Yet men in their forties and their fifties who once held powerful positions and had high gross incomes have, time and again, found themselves out of employment and unable to find another job at more than a fraction of their original income. There are placement consultants whose businesses are built on their clients' vain hopes of getting a job at even half the salary.

One method of dealing with a risk is to insure against it. That is the method of the manager who sells his service to the highest bidder. The other method, however, is to try to see that the risk doesn't happen. This latter method involves turning management from a free-for-all into a profession. Professionalism after all is not just a matter of fixing a public schedule of fees. Professionalism is a whole attitude to work and a whole relationship both of the members of the profession with each other and of the members with those they serve.

If an enterprise wants managers who are going to serve it professionally, then it had better treat them as professionals. The professional expects to be set high standards. He has a particular competence and expects that competence to be demanded of him. The professional owes a duty of care to those whom he serves, and, in turn, he expects that they will trust him and give him real responsibility and not breathe down his neck. And because the services of the professional are so important and are so difficult to judge by the standards of the market-place, society has usually given him some protection against the crudest of market pressures. Doctors are not expected to offer cut-price surgery, "Brain tumours removed for only fifty guineas."

If a business expects to get the best out of its professional management, then it must have something of the relationship with them that a professional man has with his client. It must give them a large measure of security and trust, and it must allow them largely to set their own standards, to be their own judges and, within the enterprise and its overall objectives, to set their own personal objectives. Of course, there are levels in the enterprise where this is impracticable, just as there are levels in a professional firm short of a partnership. But there comes the level in a business where, to quote a personnel director of a large American company, you cannot lay down a rigid job specification because "the man makes the job".

There should be no conflict between the objectives of the professional manager and the objectives of the enterprise. Professional management aims at optimum economic performance. What stands in the way of optimum performance is not the manager who puts his profession above the aims of the business but palace politics, pet projects, inertia, pride, and even wilfulness, which divert business from its true economic ends. Companies where these things thrive are usually the ones which also drive out professionals and end up either with incompetent managers or with management which will come only on the payment of a high risk premium.

But even as the enterprise owes a duty to its professional managers, so the manager also has an obligation upwards to those who control the enterprise. A business normally faces downwards and outwards. The firing-line is in the customer's office and on the production floor. Those in the firing-line tend to regard those above them as unproductive overheads, and find it hard to see what contribution they make to the business. The Whitehall machine (that is the law-making governmental machine rather than the parts like the Health Service, which are business in all but name) by contrast tends to face inwards and upwards. Action is taken at the centre and top by the Minister, who is accountable to Parliament. Therefore the whole machine is geared to serve the next man up. Whatever one's view about the two stances, there is no doubt that the civil servant has a much better idea of how to help his immediate boss than the manager. Just as Whitehall's relations downwards and outwards are often poor, so business's relations inwards and upwards are often poor. In most businesses most managers could spend a lot more time than they do thinking of the decisions their boss has to make and taking positive steps to help him make them well.

I find that another contrast between Whitehall and business is the much greater ability of Whitehall to abide by decisions once these are made. In both places a stupid decision will tend to be fudged, even by the most professional managers, if only to protect the department or the enterprise against the folly of its temporary rulers. However, decisions of this sort are rare, and where there has been full and free discussion and a majority verdict has been reached the decision should be carried out. Otherwise, nothing is ever settled, and no policy can ever have a firm base. Of course, one needs to be flexible, to reverse a decision which is evidently wrong. But then there should be a positive decision to be flexible or to alter policy, not just a vacuum of inertia.

The people who make the final decisions in any enterprise are the directors, and it is on them and normally on two or three of them that the whole tone and performance of the enterprise ultimately depends. It is the conduct of these men which will determine whether they have a professional management or not. These are the men who reconcile the claims made upon the enterprise by its customers, by its employees, and by its shareholders. These are the men, too, who have to reconcile any conflicting claims of public and private interest. Possibly five thousand people make these key decisions which affect the whole life and happiness of all of us—indeed, of all those who depend on us for aid, military protection, and capital investment. What society needs from these men above all is competent and professional performance. They are in charge of the industrial machine, and if this machine does not perform competently, then nothing the elected Government can do will provide the houses, schools, sick-bays, the hospitals, the old-age pensions, and the standard of living the country expects. What society demands, therefore, of the tycoon is not that he should be lovable or amusing or full of panache, but that he should perform efficiently and that he should drive and not cruise. He has the key to the nation's productive potential, and he must be certain that he uses it.

An enterprise does not exist in a vacuum. It has plant in particular towns. It is somebody's neighbour. It may export 100 per cent of its products, and be all that it should be in the national interests, but this does not absolve it from the obligation to be a good neighbour. Most big companies now take their local obligations very seriously. We have gone on a long way from the pioneering of Bournville and Port Sunlight. The dark satanic mill is no more than a memory, and smoke and effluent, although they exist, are under control. But there is still far too great a gap between the local company management and the local community. The community is still inclined to see the company as at once powerful and a bit mysterious, as something beyond its ken with which it is not easy to come to terms. Local authorities are often made up of the shopkeeper and the small trade, and where they contain professional people these are more likely to be the schoolteacher and the lawyer than the plant manager or the works engineer. I cannot help feeling that companies would do well to be more personally and directly involved in the local community. This would admittedly be hard on company management, would bring it into areas where it has had little experience and could involve acute dilemmas of conflict of interest. Nevertheless, the company still has quite a long way to go in fitting into the social framework, and this may be one of the most fruitful points of contact even if it is also one of the most difficult.

There has been a great deal of talk lately about the international company. Those who see the free operation of the market economy as the answer to all our problems are especially impatient with the limitations placed on a company by the national interest. Their idea is that the company should have the sole objective of economic performance, and they therefore rejoice at the idea of a company which is so large and so wide-spread that it rides right across frontiers and knows no trammels of national interest. In fact, the unfettered international company is a myth. Every company must have some national base. This is not only a legal necessity but a moral necessity. I remember the director of a great 'international' company complaining of the effects of corporation tax. He explained that his company had had for a good many years what is technically known as a 'nil U.K. rate' of taxation. Their U.K. tax had been offset against their tax paid overseas. In the new scheme only the corporation tax could be offset and the schedule F tax he paid to his shareholders could not. He explained that after the transitional period he would have to reduce his dividend. This he felt was unfair; he was sure that this was the last thing which had been intended. But the reply was un-sympathetic. He was told, "What you are really saying is that for all these years you have employed millions and millions of British capital, employed thousands and thousands of British citizens, had an enormous share of the British market, and yet you have paid absolutely no British taxes at all. Don't you think that it is time that the British Exchequer had just a little bit of money from you?"

Limited liability is a privilege bestowed on the company by the State. It is not a common-law right. It is created by the statute law of the country for specific purposes and with specific limitations. The State creates the legal framework in which the company can operate, and in that framework the State will protect it and see that justice is done. Citizenship has privileges and obligations, and neither company nor citizen can expect to have the one without the other.

The company also depends heavily upon society for the skills which it employs. The board may feel that they and they alone have been responsible for the profits which the company makes. Certainly, they make many of the key decisions. They can, as we have said, make or break the industrial machine. But they depend on society for the infrastructure within which they work. They depend especially on the country's educational system for producing the skills which enable them to operate at all. Indeed, the company also depends on society for the whole ethical framework within which it operates. Anyone who has travelled the world knows that this ethical framework differs sharply from country to country and that the economic performance of a company depends heavily on the honesty and willingness to work of the citizens of the countries where it operates. Even the international company depends on the ability of its Government to protect its overseas property and expatriate staff. It is all very well for companies to go to tax havens. But these tax havens depend on the protection of major powers, and that protection costs money, money which has to be found by their fellow-countrymen who are content to remain paying citizens.

Finally, the State is responsible, as all States have been from the beginning of time, for the national currency issued in its name. Although there are now international currency arrangements these are ultimately based on national currencies, and we are dependent on Government to maintain these national currencies at their full value. Without national currencies international trade could not be carried on, and there would be no international business. This entitles Governments to claim the goodwill of business in all the many actions which it takes which affect the value of the national currency.

But not only does the enterprise owe an obligation to the society which protects it and on which it is based, society also owes some obligations to the enterprise. Government is not slow to ask business to do this or that in the national interest, but business also has its claim to make.

Just as relations between people are best based on mutual respect, so relations between Government and business must be based on mutual respect. Government has ultimate power. It is sovereign. For that very reason it should exercise its power with discretion and should not bully or threaten. Governments who want their way and Governments who are in a hurry, sometimes, and for the best reasons, are inclined to hustle and find it difficult to be patient. But respect and patience are likely to get a far better response from business, and good relations between Government and business are bound to benefit society as a whole.

A good Government will give business a clear framework within which to operate, and will do its best in its management of the economy to make the interests of the business and the interests of the nation coincide. If this needs tough political decisions it will take them. It will not, by failing to take decisions, create an adverse climate and then exhort business to act against its economic interests to produce the results which Government has failed to produce. Above all, it will not call in question the framework of the market economy within which business operates.

These are ideals both for business and for Government. They can never be wholly attained, but if they cannot be attained they should be at least attempted. Both industry and Government owe it to society never to break off diplomatic relations and always to keep on trying. And in Britain, where we are unmatched in the closeness and sophistication of our industry-Government relations, we have the special duty which falls on the leader in this field to set an example which others can follow and which can set a standard of conduct for the whole world.

2 | *The Ethics of Corporate Behaviour*

by SIR PETER RUNGE

Sir Peter Runge was born in 1909 and was educated at Charterhouse and Oxford, where he obtained an honours degree in chemistry. He joined Tate and Lyle in 1931, was appointed to the board in 1936, and became Joint Vice-Chairman in 1958. He was appointed President of the Federation of British Industries in 1963 and Vice-President of the Confederation of British Industry in 1965. Sir Peter was a member of the National Economic Development Council 1964–66, is Chairman of the Industrial Society, a Director of Vickers, and Chairman of the British National Export Council.

Questions about ethics are never easy, and questions about ethics in industry are no exception. I think that this may be because, of all subjects, those involving ethics lend themselves the least readily to arguing from the general to the particular. Perhaps this is why the admirable statement of principles on social and industrial relations known as the Marlow Declaration has not been developed. I don't say that it is impossible to lay down principles—indeed, I shall be advocating the drawing up of codes of practice—but it is easier to do so on a narrow front. In these ethical issues one must, I am sure, acknowledge that circumstances *do* alter cases. One even has a sneaking feeling of sympathy for the costermonger's son who, before committing himself to answering his infant school's mathematics teacher on what two and two made, wanted to know whether he was a buyer or a seller.

While I was preparing this contribution, I had it in mind to call it "Corporate Dishonesty" and to make my general theme the progressive lowering of standards with increasing anonymity—this, I should add, was against the advice of some of my friends who thought my flippancy might be misunderstood—but I happened to read a syndicated article in my parish magazine which made me wonder whether I had taken the right decision. It was called "A New Look at Sin". It pointed the moral that men could become trapped in a system against their wills. It took as its example the mythical Sir Alfred Slateye, a very successful businessman given to the difficult feat of stabbing competitors in the back over the telephone, who, we could see from a drawing, was a diabolic, compulsive money-grabber, with "a peculiar kind of cold greyness in his eyes which always look like small pieces of bluey-grey slate".

Sir Alfred was not a hard worker; his office hours were 10.30 to 4.15, and he held views about industrial spying, a phrase which he said meant the employment of a firm of people to steal industrial secrets. It was legal, he said, common practice, and an essential part of healthy competition. His retort on being asked what he felt about the ethics of all that sort of thing was, "Ethics, my dear young man, there's no room for ethics in business".

I must say it shook me. The article, which was not supposed to be funny, was to my way of thinking guilty of gross misrepresentation and set out to give the impression that business practice was the eighth deadly sin; and it was being served up to a readership comprising one of the most responsible sections of the community. It made me wonder whether, after all, instead of probing into the shortcomings of industry, it would be better to defend its practices.

However, caricatures do serve to remind one that there is such a thing as smugness, and what can be more unattractive than that? Like other things one's best friends won't tell one about, one can be unconscious of it. There is a Latin tag which I have salvaged from misspent schooldays that goes, *Quod non est simulo, dissimuloque quod est*, which can be freely translated as "I don false feathers to mask the truth". We are probably all guilty sometimes, and to some extent, of acting a part, but it is a dangerous game and one that can too easily lead to self-delusion. It is certainly not the way of creating what public relations experts call a good image. Straightforwardness is not only to be preferred but is infinitely more effective than prevarication and half-truths. Not that I am advocating the indiscriminate use of the brutal truth. I don't count diplomatic language or, come to that, white lies as prevarication. There is no need to cause pain in order to be frank.

It is a temptation to justify deviousness, if not deceit and deception, as the means towards achieving an acceptable end.

In one's personal life they very seldom do, and I suspect that this is so in one's business life as well. Curiously enough, in this connection I have sympathy for politicians who can only do what they think is *acceptable*—acceptable, that is to say, to the electorate—not what they think is *right*. This must inevitably lead to imputations of insincerity, but I have it in my heart to forgive them for it. I must admit, however, to an extreme dislike of the practice of some politicians in the western world, and almost all politicians in the developing world, of being friendly in private and abusive in public. Nor can I stomach the view that it was a triumph for French diplomacy to be able to persuade the Egyptians that they had stood aloof from the Arab-Israel war of 1967, when the Egyptian Air Force had been destroyed exclusively by French aircraft.

These are affairs, however, outside our present purpose. I mention them only to point my arguments. Our main concern is with industry. We have to face the fact that the industrial way of life doesn't stand very high in the esteem of people of the academic world, of the professions, or of the services, nor, I suspect, of the Church. Industry, of course, lacks the romance of agriculture with its haymaking and sweet-smelling fields of beans or of the merchant service with its duty-free cigarettes and girls in every port. But this by no means accounts fully for its lack of favours.

We must look beyond the superficialities. I believe that the reasons, though in part sociological in character, are largely concerned with ethical or moral values. And the whole issue is a squidgy mass of ignorance, taboo, and prejudice.

Industry has, I fear, the image of Dives. People mistrust the incentives of profit and personal gain, and they shrink from the effects that these incentives, together with the spur of competition, have on behaviour. Profit is particularly marked out for attack.

There is, of course, a lot of woolly thinking about profit. Even when using it colloquially we haven't made up our minds whether it is nice or dirty. We refer to a "nice little profit" in one breath, and in the next line will run someone down with some such expression as "He's a quick-profit man", or be downright abusive by calling him a profiteer. There is no clear line dividing nice profit from nasty profit. It is a spectrum with fuzzy edges in which you take up your position according to your political beliefs, your religious convictions, the greenness of your eyes, or the side of the bed out of which you got in the morning. At one end profits are desirable and ethical; at the other they are unwanted and wicked.

But this imprecision is not confined to colloquialisms. In serious-thinking circles there is a grave lack of understanding of the profit motive. I believe this most likely stems from a lack of appreciation of the multiple role that it plays in industrial affairs, or, for that matter, in any enterprise. It plays four roles—as an incentive to create capital, as an incentive to endeavour, as a measure of efficiency, and as a test of worthwhileness.

I don't think it is difficult to defend profit in its first three roles, though a word perhaps is called for on the incentive to endeavour. Some religious writers equate personal ambition with avarice. No doubt some ambitions *are* avaricious in nature, but this is not to say that a desire to better one's own lot and that of one's children is to be deplored. Indeed, it should be encouraged. I personally don't believe in the sentiments of the third verse of *All things bright and beautiful*:

> The rich man in his castle,
> The poor man at his gate,
> God made them high or lowly,
> And ordered their estate.

It is when we come to the last role—the test of worthwhileness—that we are on treacherous ground. From a technical point of view profit is often the indispensable measure for determining priorities. Frequently the only criterion, for example, that can be applied by management to determine whether to invest in one project rather than another, whether to invest now or next year, or whether to invest at all, is that of potential profit.

On broader issues, however, above the technical level things are not so simple. Few people, if anyone, it is true, would maintain that a fat profit makes a striptease show more worth while than ballet with its thin one, or that shoddiness and bad taste can be justified by the profits they may earn. But such examples are extremes, and there is no gainsaying that in less obvious cases there is room for differences of opinion about the extent that the incentive of material gain may warp our sense of values. Take one-armed bandits, for instance. There are some who would say that for the profit motive to encourage the manufacture of machines which exploit the gambling instinct is bad, perhaps even wicked. There are others who see nothing wrong in it at all.

Or take my own business of sugar. No harm in that, you would say. But what about the by-product of rum—that's not everyone's cup of tea. There must be many people who disapprove of making profits from alcoholic drinks. It would not even be surprising if from time to time there was a member of our board who was uneasy about it. But what is he expected to do? He is in the minority. There may be a moral issue involved where he personally is concerned, but not in the community generally. He is forced to suppress his own feelings and conform with the majority. And in my view he is right to do so.

I give this example to show that the standards of groups must be more of a compromise than those of individuals. The danger lies in compromise developing into licence. The larger the group the greater this danger is, and in addition one has to deal with the effects of anonymity. I fear that it is a common weakness to feel strongly only about those things which affect one's personal reputation. The ethics of the village carpenter, blacksmith, or shopkeeper don't cause them sleepless nights. They are dictated, to put it at its lowest, by self-interest and self-preservation. Their personal reputations are at stake. If their behaviour does not come up to the standards that village opinion expects they lose business—perhaps go out of business.

It is a different matter with corporations. With them there are no personal reputations at stake. Even though the head of a business is a public figure, he is not held personally responsible for the actions of his managers. And so we find that boards of directors are prepared to take joint decisions of a nature which perhaps not one of them individually would care to do.

One might incidentally note that even an individual's approach to ethics is conditioned by the size of the stakes. I have no doubt that Henrietta Maria was strictly honourable domestically, but she was happy to advise her son, Charles II,

"You must not think it necessary to keep any treaties further than they may serve your ends".

Anonymity encourages a lowering of standards in both directions. Many an upright citizen has persuaded himself that railways are fair game. Children delight in working out schemes that will allow them to travel free. In the same vein I remember once thanking a lorry-driver for reporting a theft of sugar from our warehouse. He was embarrassed at being thanked and said, "That's all right, Guv; after all it's not like the docks—the sugar *belongs* to someone here".

The ultimate in anonymity is the Civil Service, and I have no doubt that we can all think of examples where this has led to questionable behaviour. And no doubt we all have our little hates. Mine concerns the tendency of bureaucracy to yield to importunity. There is the thick-file theory, which holds that you only get your way when the to-and-fro correspondence can no longer be threaded on to the lace of standard length.

It is not, however, my object to discuss the public's mistrust of officialdom, and man's conviction that there is no milk of human kindness in the heart of a tax-gatherer. But that shafts are aimed at public services as well as at industry is a clear indication that it is not profit alone which breeds mistrust; there are other powerful factors, amongst which the impersonality of large organizations ranks very high.

And yet, in spite of its anonymity, one must notice that nobody ever accuses the law of being unjust (sometimes it is dubbed unfair) and that discipline in the armed services very seldom produces mutinies. I wonder whether this perhaps is due to the complete documentation of the rules in both those organizations.

It is, of course, impossible to discuss the ethics of competitive industry without considering the conflict which may exist between private gain and public interest. If one believes—and many sincere people do—that competition and market forces will in the long run ensure automatically that the sum of all individual effort will bring maximum benefit to the community as a whole, that is an end to the question. For myself, I believe that, although this may well be true in primitive economies, it is not true in our own state of development, and that individuals as persons or corporations should look farther than their own immediate gain when making both long-term and short-term decisions.

It is fair, of course, to ask what criteria should be applied if private gain is to be subordinated to something else. In personal decisions what is acceptable can only be dictated by one's faith, one's upbringing, and one's conscience. Logical argument can help, but it cannot alone decide. And this also applies to an individual taking part in a collective decision. Compromise, as I have pointed out earlier, is the corollary to collective decisions, and there is no harm in that, but there comes a point when one decides that one cannot sell one's soul. Someone once said to me that no-one is worth his salt who hasn't threatened to resign on a matter of principle at least once in his career. I don't know whether I go quite as far as that, but I can see what he meant. The man who always votes with the chair doesn't make much of a contribution. I myself, incidentally, do *just* qualify by his test for the élite.

But let me return to the public interest. It can be broadly divided between the sociological and the economic interest of the nation as a whole. An example of the first which springs to mind where conflict can arise is advertising. Let me say straight out that I see nothing conceivably wrong in promoting the sale of goods or services if their use is allowed by law and they are acceptable to the religious beliefs of the majority.

It must be remembered that the encouragement of consumption can take many forms. What I want to emphasize is that posters and commercials on the television are not the only weapons in the marketeer's armoury. Manufacturers will choose the cheapest method available to achieve their aim. One way of promoting the sale of goods, for instance, is by giving large margins to retailers and leaving it to them to persuade people to buy. Another is to advertise and thus persuade people to *demand* special brands. The retailer will then reduce his margin to encourage people into his shop. In both cases the ultimate purchaser has been persuaded to buy, and he has had to pay something for having been persuaded. There is to my mind no ethical preference for one method or the other.

Where there is room for controversy it is in the way the advertising is carried out. Untrue or misleading descriptions and preying on fear or prejudice are the sort of practices which should be condemned. It is interesting and encouraging that the advertising industry has not found it difficult to make a list of objectionable practices and voluntarily put a stop to them by persuasion.

One can see from this that in advertising, as in so many other spheres, individuals and groups are perfectly prepared—indeed, are anxious—to adopt high standards so long as they can feel sure that another of their number is not going to gain advantage as a result of their own abstention.

Promotion of sales is an example where material standards can come into conflict with moral standards, but the public interest is not only concerned with moral issues. There is as well the economic interest of the nation. That too has to engage the attention of the private sector of industry. There is a special case where foreign trade is concerned. The question is whether undertakings in the private sector have a national duty to try to export their manufactures. Frankly I don't think small or even medium-sized concerns do have such a duty, but I think they are pretty supine if they don't have a shot at it. Larger concerns, however, do, I believe, have to take the national interest into their calculations when deciding what resources to allocate to their export effort. They have a responsibility in this, just as they have in not despoiling the countryside with slag heaps or in deforestation or in polluting rivers or, in the agricultural field, in soil mining. But if you ask me to quantify these responsibilities I cannot do so.

Finally in this area of conflicting interests there is the question of trading with countries whose internal policies are open to criticism on moral grounds. In this my mind is made up. It is not for individual companies to decide whether to exercise private sanctions. A shopkeeper serves rogues and saints indiscriminately—indeed, in some cases he is forced by law to do so. An exporter should take his cue from that. I am conscious, led me add, of not being the first person to take this view.

I have purposely kept away from discussing the ethics of trade-union practice. For one thing it is not my subject, and for another circumstances alter cases in this field too. I am not prepared lightly to condemn or defend. Nevertheless, the subject is important. Just as management has much to answer for, so have labour leaders. And the conflicts between private gain and public interest are just as difficult for them to resolve as they are for others. Wage restraint, bullying tactics in negotiations, coercion to conform by declaring a closed shop are all issues about which there is plenty to be said.

There is one extremely important and difficult angle to do with labour relations generally which I must mention. Sociologists tell us that group loyalties are strongest if there is an enemy; and some observers think that the importance of solidarity to workpeople is itself often a main cause for groups failing to co-operate with authority. To sympathize with the boss is to cut the bonds which create the groups. If this is so we have an uphill task in front of us. But it is a generality, and, as I have said before, in such matters it is a mistake to argue from the general to the particular.

There is one thing only about which I would like to be specific. It is the nature of a contract when it is made between master and man or between management and trade union. One set of people sees no difference between such a contract and any other. Its sanctity is undiminished just because it involves human beings. At the other extreme another set sees in it no more than a declaration of intent to be kept or broken as circumstances make expedient (but not, I fancy, to be broken by management). For myself, I find both extremes wrong. I don't think that one can hold that labour contracts are in fact made between equals. They must surely, therefore, be subject to different rules from those that regulate commercial contracts. On the other hand an agreement with no sanctions if it is broken is an absurdity. I believe we must put the present state of affairs right. As things stand, honourable men apparently gaily break their words, and this does them no good, the trade union movement no good and industry no good either.

That brings me to an end to what I have to say. What conclusions can we draw from it all? Certainly that the standards of corporations are the subject of compromise, and are, therefore, unlikely to be as high or, come to that, as debased as those of individuals. Certainly that anonymity leads to a lowering of standards. But we needn't despair; corporations are not entirely unprincipled. Just as is the case with persons, they prefer high standards if there is general conformity to them. To help them codes of practice can be drawn up such as has been done for advertising and certain Stock Exchange transactions.

We conclude perhaps that we cannot apply a rigid set of principles to all industrial behaviour; that circumstances *do* alter cases. But we can also conclude that moral values are not irreconcilable with material values. Certainly there are many men of the highest principles who are engaged in industry and commerce who find in its materialism a great challenge and feel that they are making a major contribution to society by promoting its efficiency. They have absolutely no feeling of guilt.

We find it difficult to prescribe a test for examining one's own behaviour. One's conscience must be the judge. Straightforwardness and sincerity perhaps are the key words; and I might add consistency. Fairness, too, is important, but this often means giving no more to one than to others. A dismal fact as old as the parable of the vineyard.

And the cure? Patience above all. Never despair. And if there is a single aspect to mention on which to concentrate it is communications. No effort is too great to achieve understanding of the reasoning behind policies and decisions. Ignorance is the great enemy. The cynic says that God gave man the power of speech to hide his thoughts, but He also gave it to him as a means of exercising leadership. One is tempted sometimes to think that in this large-scale modern world the individual has ceased to count. It isn't so. The vast majority of men and women are crying out for leadership. Don't let people who are in a position to do so be frightened of giving it. And let them be prepared to be held accountable for their individual and corporate actions. They should never be ashamed of a decision to which they have been party. Let them stand forth and be counted.

3 | Company Director:

Rights and Responsibilities

by ERIC FOSTER

Eric Foster was born in 1913. He was educated at King's School, Rochester. He has spent the whole of his working life in journalism except for 1940–46, when he served in the Royal Navy, emerging as a Lieutenant-Commander, R.N.V.R. He was Editor of the *Director* from 1949 to 1966, when he became Editor-in-Chief. He is a part-time director of the British School of Motoring and associated companies. He is married, with two children. His interests include golf, family life, and conversation.

"A directorship is in that stage of professionalism where there is no official recognition or designation of standards other than in the strictly legal and often necessarily narrow sense of the Companies Act." This was written in the Institute of Directors' publication *Standard Boardroom Practice* before recent legislation circumscribed still more closely the freedom of action of the company director, but it still stands. Standards of behaviour followed by the majority of directors in the United Kingdom still range far outside what is controlled by legislation, even though 'professionalism', clearly, is increasingly a characteristic of the director today.

The future may well see attempts to form directors into a professional group, to which admittance would depend on qualifying examinations and adherence to centrally defined codes of behaviour, although it is not easy to see how this evolution would take place. For the moment, and this represents positive gains for commercial flexibility and economic growth, the "profession" is open to all, and in large areas of business life each director is free to make his own rules.

The result is that directors form an extraordinarily diversi-fied group, ranging from men with little formal education to executives with professional qualifications and higher degrees and from the chairmen of boards responsible for hundreds of millions of pounds of capital investment and thousands of employees to men starting up in business for the first time in a small way.

But, no matter what his background or his financial resources may be, the director has responsibilities as exacting and often as precise as those carried by the members of the professions. If the sanctions of the law are not always operative, none the less conscience, instinct, self-advantage, and the remorseless pressure of public opinion expressed through the Press or the shareholders succeed remarkably effectively in maintaining among directors generally a high regard for these responsibilities. From reading the newspapers it is easy to misjudge the incidence of roguery among directors. Perhaps because the title 'director' implies, in the public mind, wealth and power, it needs only a slight slip by a director to get unusual attention in the Press. "Director on dangerous-driving charge" justly commands more reader interest than "Greengrocer on dangerous-driving charge", although, with the proliferation of tiny man-and-wife companies, the greengrocer and the director may well be one and the same person.

Where problems arise it is mostly not because of any irresponsibility on the part of the director, but because of a lack of certainty about where his responsibilities lie as between sometimes conflicting interests in particular circumstances. The general rule is clear enough, but its application is not always so sure.

The general rule is this: that the first and paramount responsibility of the director is towards the company which he serves. The considerations opened up by this statement are very wide-ranging, but it will help to illustrate its significance, to start with, by considering the active day-to-day role of the company director as a member of the board. In many large and in most smaller companies the executive has a dual function within the organization, serving it both in his capacity as a director of the company and in his functional role, which carries with it specific responsibilities for sales, production, or research and development, and so forth. Outside the boardroom his functional role is uppermost, not that common sense will not dictate that he keep the interests of other departments constantly in mind; once he is in the boardroom, he must discard his departmental or functional aims and attitudes and view the problems presented to him from the standpoint of the company as a whole.

Here is the crucial distinction, therefore, between the role of the manager as such and the role of the director. Nowadays (and the trend will become far more pronounced as business studies are extended in Britain) more and more directors are highly competent managers, specializing in functional areas with which their own enthusiasms and aspirations naturally tend to become identified. But their role in this context is quite distinct from the part they play as members of the board. In the boardroom they are responsible for the overall well being of the company they serve; their task is to give their approval to the policy suggestions that may come up from management and to ensure that the company is in a position to carry them through. With today's heavy emphasis on the need for management skills and academic knowledge in business, useful as these are, the role of the director risks being confused with that of the manager: and the result is a loss for business, not least in clear-sightedness about company objectives. The point was brought out pungently by Lord Beeching, who was quoted by Mr Gerard Fiennes in *I Tried to Run a Railway* as saying, "The most difficult transition in industry is from management to direction."

The traditional and still valid 'structure' of the limited-liability company was described by Lord Chandos a few years ago, speaking to the Institute of Directors' Annual Conference, in these terms:

Business and industry consist of direction, management and workers. It is the task of the directors and not of the management to decide when plants have to be expanded, when new products have to be developed and manufactured and marketed and what risks should be taken, what credit should be extended, and so forth. In trying to make up their minds they would be right to take as much advice as they can from everybody engaged in the industry, but that is their plain responsibility which they cannot escape . . . no amount of good management can offset fundamental mistakes in direction.

The director's view is like that of Machiavelli's Prince: from the mountain-top, in terms of responsibility and vision. The function of 'direction' is perhaps seen at its purest in the non-executive or part-time director: an often abused man who none the less can bring together both a dispassionate view of the company's business and a familiarity with external factors likely to affect its development, which are invaluable. Like the other directors of the board, the part-time director, no matter by what section of the shareholders he may have been elected, must give advice in the interests of the company as a whole.

But the company itself, of course, legally an entity, is composed of various interests, shareholders, workers, and executives; is itself responsible to outside interests, notably its creditors, its customers, and the community or the State; and, moreover, is an organism with a future as well as a present. All these considerations complicate the question of where the director's responsibilities lie.

If we take the simple proposition that the director is responsible for the overall well-being of the company, forgetting for the moment the often conflicting interests involved, we must then look at the question of the main purpose of the company which absorbs his attention and energies. And lately, of course, under the twin pressures of national need and American example, the gospel has been increasingly preached and accepted that the role of the company is to make profits. The position was put very clearly by Lord Beeching, in a talk at the London School of Economics and Political Science, in which the aim of the private company was defined chiefly by contrasting its purpose with that of the nationalized industries. The objectives of a nationalized industry, Lord Beeching commented, were more numerous, more ambiguous, and less distinguishable from qualifying conditions than those of the private company: they fluctuated in their supposed order of priority not only from Government to Government and year to year but almost from day to day. "In this confused situation, top management of nationalized industries have to create their own clarity and continuity of purpose . . ." In contrast, the primary objective of any company in the private sector was "to make the best possible return on the capital provided by the shareholders . . . also, in order to be able to conduct its business well in the present and safeguard its future, it must have regard to established practices and public opinion about the social desirability of its activities".

The director's primary duty to ensure that the company he serves is built up into an enterprise of high and sustained profitability may largely require him to take decisions where technical competence and common sense alone provide the answers he needs when there seems to be a clash between the interests of the company and the interests of, say, the shareholders or the company's workers. There is bound to be a constant tension. Thus on the whole, but not always, shareholders and workers prefer jam today rather than jam tomorrow. It is for the board to bear the time factor in mind: the long-term needs of the company will decide what amount of the profits to allocate to reserves, what amount to distribute in dividends. And in this context it is worth making the important distinction between being a representative and being a delegate. The director is and must remember that he is the former. As a representative of the shareholders he must exercise his own judgment. What he decides may not always be in the immediate future interests of the shareholders, but if it is in the interests of the company over a longer period, the director will be vindicated. If, through a fault in judgment, he proves to have been wrong and the company suffers in consequence, then the remedy, of course, is in the shareholders' hands.

More difficult problems arise when the director has the responsibility of taking decisions that qualitatively affect the future of the company and depend on questions of fundamental principle rather than technical or financial assessments. This is an area where the "best practice" rather than any written rules provides directors with guidance as to what is or is not within their powers. Again to quote from *Standard Boardroom Practice*:

> If a shareholder has invested his money in a company which, for example, is in the motor industry and the suggestion is before the board that the company should go into, say, the newspaper business, then the shareholder has a moral right to be consulted. On the other hand, if the board decides to spend a considerable sum of money on re-equipment which will increase production or make it more efficient, then that is the responsibility of the directors.

Now that the word 'moral' has crept in, one has to face the wide and almost treacherous problem of discussing 'business ethics' in a meaningful way. At one extreme the director would accept that business life is not exempt from any of the ethical considerations that govern the behaviour of individuals in their private conduct. At the other extreme the professions and the State lay down laws and regulations which, just like any other citizen subscribing to a professional code or managing his affairs in accord with the law, he is bound to observe. In between, however, there is a very large area indeed where decisions are not so easy to make and responsibilities not so clear. Nor can they easily be ascertained by reference to the 'good of the company' or the pursuit of profitability.

At the Institute of Directors' Conference in 1966 Cardinal Heenan was asked whether he would give his reflections on the 'morality' of take-over bids. He replied as follows:

> If I said anything important this morning it was this, that you must forget the slogan 'business is business', if you mean that you will justify sharp practice in the name of business. Profit is not everything.
> You can take a small business which has been in a family for years and generations, and not only owned by a family but the employees have belonged to the same families for generations; they have grown up knowing that Smith & Smith & Smith & Sons are their bread and butter. Their loyalty has been to Smith & Smith & Smith & Sons before anything else.
> If in 1969 one of the miserable young Smiths who has come into the business finds he can do a quick deal and get rid of all that and all the worry, knowing that his firm is being bought up for destruction and not for expansion; if he makes a deal without having any legal safeguard for all those people who have given their lives and their fathers before them, then I say that is immoral.

Nothing, at first sight, could be more exact or fairer; and on this point the Cardinal clearly carried his audience, of over five thousand shrewd and hard-headed businessmen, all the way with him. But are circumstances always so weighted in favour of the director's taking what is clearly the right decision? The instance postulated by the Cardinal, disregarding the 'family' nature of the business, boils down in essence to the moral duty of a director to regard the welfare of his employees as coming within the sphere of his broad responsibilities to the *company*—an entity which includes employees as well as shareholders and demands thought for the morrow as well as today. It is clearly immoral to throw men on to the streets and to cause their destitution by lack of foresight and refusal to make arrangements for them when negotiating for the take-over of a company. But how is one to draw the line when it comes to allocating the money available between compensation for the shareholders and provision for the employees?

In this context, incidentally, there has been a remarkable shift in public sentiment during the past twenty years: when the 'classic' take-over bids of the 1950's were hitting the headlines, public, and even business and Whitehall, sympathies were usually with the defending board. It was, indeed, thought even immoral to seize by these means a company in order to make more efficient use of its assets or dispose of them for cash, in turn to be put to better uses. Times change, and today the beneficial and wholesome nature of mergers and amalgamations is fully accepted. Pressing economic needs have brought about a transformation in the moral climate, and this inevitably affects the way directors regard their business.

Moreover, the range of a director's responsibilities has during the same period of time been subtly extended, not only by increasing emphasis on his duty to make sure that his company is truly profitable, but also by the growing insistence that to be in business is to be doing a form of national service, where one's inefficiency is not a matter for oneself alone, or even one's shareholders, but for the country as a whole. As medieval traders were pilloried for selling shoddy goods, today's director finds himself denounced not for sharp dealing but for failing to make his company grow. This has practical consequences, in fact if not in law, tending to force on boardrooms an awareness of the consequences for the State as well as for their individual companies of whatever decisions they may take. And the possibilities of conflicting demands become all the greater.

The chase after higher profits can never take the place of regard for the total well-being of the company which has emerged, in practice, as the prime responsibility of the company director. As we have seen, in carrying this responsibility the

D

director cannot always find laws and rules to make his mind up for him. Common sense and common decency often provide the answers. Above all, he needs what is nowadays the supreme business virtue: judgment. In management, as the 'professionals' point out, the area of decision-making covered by 'hunch' or 'judgment' is still larger by far than that where automatic, scientific approaches are possible. In management, however, science is gradually making inroads into judgment. In the direction of companies the same process is at work: but there will always remain a wide and vital area where the director's judgment must reign supreme. There will always be a moment where the director—or, more properly, the board as a whole—must say 'yes' or 'no' as the issues consequent on this judgment can be enormous—for good or evil. It is in exercising this judgment that the director will always recall these words of Lord Shawcross: "It is a wise rule for a director never to acquiesce in his company doing anything which done by an individual he would consider shabby or impermissible." In that single sentence lies the heart of the whole matter.

4 | *Industry and Government*

by JOHN DAVIES

John Davies was appointed the first Director-General of the new CBI in August 1965. To this role he brought his experience of fifteen years in the oil industry, during which time he became the chief executive of the biggest oil-marketing and -distributing organization in Western Europe.

Born on January 8th, 1916, he was educated at Windlesham House School, Sussex, and St Edward's School, Oxford. After training as a chartered accountant he audited accounts in many parts of Europe. During the War he served first in the 9th Armoured Division and then transferred to the Staff of the Combined Operations Experimental Establishment. In 1946 he joined the Anglo-Iranian Oil Company (now the British Petroleum Company), and he became Managing Director of Shell-Mex and B.P. in 1961, and subsequently was appointed Vice-Chairman and Managing Director.

John Davies is a member of the National Economic Development Council, the Council of Industrial Design, the National Joint Advisory Council to the Department of Employment and Productivity, the Public Schools Commission, and the Council of the University of Sussex. He is the Vice-President of Political and Economic Planning, and is, in addition, a Fellow of the Royal Society of Arts and a Governor of the National Institute of Economic and Social Research.

The time which has elapsed since the birth of CBI on August 1st, 1965, has proved a period—if ever there was one—when the full depths of Government/industrial relations have been plumbed—or, if that sounds too critical a way of expressing it, then perhaps I might say the full length has been measured. In this essay I propose to stand back briefly from the hurly-burly and try and gain some perspective of this wide field not only to achieve thereby a sense of balance but, no less, to see whether this period has taught one anything in the way of detecting improvements or suggesting changes.

A little analysis is always a good beginning, so I start by trying to fit into some realistic framework the main areas where industry finds itself at grips with Government. In the nature of

51

things such a framework needs to be devised in Government rather than in industrial terms since, for the most part, Government has proved itself more disposed to intervene in industry rather than vice versa, a fact concerning which industrialists would do well to be less resigned. My analysis shows Government involved with industry in a number of quite different guises.

(1) *As a protector of the people* in the sense that it is concerned, among many other things, with restraining industry from damaging the people by polluting their air and water; by injuriously invading their living and recreational areas; by abusing, through excessive market power, their rights as customers; by treating them harshly as workpeople; by harming their interests as shareholders; and so on in many varied fields.

(2) *As a provider of services* of widespread and varied kinds. Post and telecommunications; transport both as to the infrastructure and as to operating facilities; safeguarding services concerned with health, police, protection from fire; energy services; education services; labour-exchange services.

(3) *As a customer* responsible for expenditure of more than 40 per cent of the value of everything the nation produces and touching thereby every sector of industry and commerce.

(4) *As an industrialist* managing vast industries like electricity, gas, railways, and many others—competing with private industry for customers and resources, faced with so many of the same industrial problems in labour relations, in research, in design and so many more matters.

(5) *As a maker of foreign policy*, not only in the field of trading agreements but also in that of international social relationships with all their immense impact upon international trade.

And finally

(6) *As a manager of the nation's resources*, and it is with this characteristic that I would like principally to deal here.

I detect some clear stages in Government's own appreciation of its role in this field. For centuries its sole concern is that there should be available to it by taxation or other acquisitive methods sufficient to enable the objectives of policy to be achieved. Wars must be won; colonies established; intrusive foreigners repulsed; armies maintained; public buildings ornamented; and resources must be forthcoming accordingly. Where they come from and why is not at that stage the concern of Government, which has nobler, vaguer, and often more bloody purposes with which to concern itself.

A new stage is reached when Government is confronted with the absence of resources or the risk of absence, arising from external causes. It is alerted to the risk of non-fulfilment of its objectives and becomes involved in the correction of these tendencies by the powers it possesses. Taxation ceases to be only a means of levying the resources it needs and becomes a protective mechanism against foreign industrial invasion. Colonial development becomes the means of procurement of raw materials. By the end of the nineteenth century this stage was well established.

Yet another great step is taken when Government realizes that it has a role to play regarding national resources it does *not* itself require. It has for centuries been accustomed to appropriating those it did; it has recently accepted the need to safeguard the existence of those it might have need of; and now it realizes that the manipulation of the whole is really in its hands and can be adapted to the social purposes it embraces. A new stride forward has taken place and a new stage has been reached: it can and will henceforward use its powers for the apportionment of resources in line with its social policies. Here in Britain we have been reconciled to such a role of Government for a generation or more and, despite the inevitable hostility of those who suffered rather than gained by apportionment, have accepted that it is a proper role, providing it is undertaken competently. As far as industry is concerned competence is seen as consistency and comprehensibility adding up to a stimulating and stable economic framework within which enterprise can flourish without undue interference. I believe that today the vast majority of private businessmen agree that this stage corresponds to their idea of a proper relationship between Government and industry—the former confining itself to constructing the cornu—and the latter filling it with the copia, if I may so describe the process.

And yet already for a decade and more a new stride has been taken and a new stage of development has been encountered. Now Government senses that it is not enough to appropriate, to safeguard, and to apportion, but believes more and more certainly that it has a leading part to play in the *creation* of national resources. As the safeguarding activity was occasioned by awareness of the risk of deprivation, and as apportionment was brought about by the pressures of social justice, so this new step is taken under the pressure of events. Now it is not a question of taking steps to protect individual resources against extinction, since the issue is clearly posed by the threat of a shortfall of total resources to fulfil the Government's policies—the trouble arises as a result of there being not enough resources to apportion.

Fired with a great enthusiasm for its new range of action, Government surveys its existing fields of work to see in what way they can be attuned to this new purpose.

1. It realizes that its taxation policies, hitherto conceived with the dual objective of fund-raising for its own purposes and adjusting the natural disposition of wealth to its social objectives, can also serve in fostering by contrast the development of one industry in preference to another; in rewarding success or enterprise or research or investment by penalizing less in a tax sense; in directing industrial effort to areas chosen by it as offering more potential than others.

2. It finds that its policies concerning employment too are susceptible to adjustment in favour of the creation of resources. The scale and nature of redundancy payments, sickness and unemployment benefits, labour-exchange activities, training in employment—all can contribute to its ideas for reorientating manpower and improving skill.

3. Housing and education policies too can be seen as falling into this broad field of action. Without diminishing the social objectives they are to achieve they also can be bent and shaped to encourage the production of resources.

4. Its international aims can be subtly swung towards the securing of resources where they are wanted: trade no longer follows the flag, but tends to precede it. Even foreign missions, with nostalgic backward glances to the high old days of real

diplomacy, are dragooned into the act and find themselves retrained as salesmen.

5. External trade bargaining ceases to be fashioned from the clay of protection on the wheel of high purpose and is seen as the vehicle for nagging and cajoling out higher resources by threats of keener competition and promises of honours and rewards of all kinds.

6. Public procurement suddenly takes on quite a new light. It ceases to be a matter of drawing a shrouding cloak of economy over the mass of confusion and imprecision and is now seen as a means of prodding the inefficient; changing the conservative; rewarding the ingenious; stimulating the imaginative; penalizing the pusillanimous; and all in the name of higher production and more rapid technological change.

7. Monetary policy, no less, is abstracted from the hands of those grey eminences practising a complex and recondite art and turned over to those newly aware of the part it too can play in nudging the hesitant.

I believe I could continue analysing each facet of Government activity and, in practically everyone, detect some element which suddenly gleams in a new colour as it is transformed by the touchstone of the desire to increase national resources. The emphasis in transport, energy, or agriculture is too obvious to warrant mention: even such things as the recruitment of the army or the police are remotely but effectively involved: the requirements of justice are not less to be debated in the context of national production.

Government with mounting zeal has embraced this new dimension and has thrown itself headlong into the struggle for higher production. Not altogether surprisingly it has found itself impelled to much criticism of those who, at the lowly scale of the enterprise—be they management or unions—have apparently failed to grasp the ease with which it should be possible to achieve more production by the introduction of a little political exhortation and logic into their affairs. Perhaps there is more than a little justice in these criticisms, but perhaps there is more than a little naïveté too.

Of course, Government recognizes that it is not possible in one single enthusiastic bound to encompass the whole spectrum of industrial knowledge—or, even if it is possible, it is wiser not to boast of it too openly. Consequently it sets about building a veritable mass of consultative groupings, conceived with the dual objective of genuinely acquiring knowledge of the workings of industry on the one side and, on the other, of quieting fears that it may be preparing to act in an arbitrary or impulsive manner.

Industrial management has at first greeted this consultative initiative with acclaim. Here at last is Government genuinely trying to understand the industrial world. The welcome stems, however, from erroneous assumption, and when the error is perceived there is disenchantment. Management had assumed that what was afoot was Government conscientiously seeking to improve and refine that framework wherein productive enterprise might prosper, whereas, in fact, what they were witnessing was Government getting in on the act. Government was involving itself in the only way it understood—namely, that of isolating individual strands of the texture of industry and seeking to strengthen or weaken them as its own convictions of what was good for industry demanded. Perhaps it is in this that the alliance of political exhortation and ruthless logic has been the most deceptive, failing as it does to capture and understand the whole complexity of the interplay of innumerable elements in the weaving of the industrial texture: the warp of profit and market forces and prices and marketing and management; and the weft of labour and raw materials and research and inspection and standards. And particularly perhaps has Government in its interventionist mood misunderstood the binding force of the respect of contracts—not observed for some quaint Quixotry derived from anachronistic paternalism, but deeply rooted in the whole structure of industry. So too has Government's vaunted precocity fallen short in giving it understanding in the time-scale of industry and the great divide which separates it from that of Government—a divide which continually deepens and widens with the ever-increasing sophistication of industry's investment planning contrasted with the ever more intensive concern of Government with its day-to-day popular image.

Here, then, we stand today—or so it seems to me—gazing with some disillusionment at one another: Government perplexed that its benevolent enthusiasm should be so lukewarmly welcomed, and management vexed to find that all that is expected of it is maximum disclosure but no participation in decision. Of course, this is not univerally the case, and some happy examples of common enterprise are to be found, but, in general, I sense a mood of resentment on both sides which must be relieved if we jointly are to realize the potential of our remarkable country.

Perhaps nowhere is this *malaise* more evident than in those twin activities where Government started on its creative course with no arrows in the quiver. Such was the case both as regards national economic planning and incomes policy. In both the initial concept was one of voluntary and collaborative action, and now, in both, the development has been in favour of autonomous Government action, with industry at best a dubious onlooker. How tragic it is that these twin cornerstones of our survival as a race, capable of contributing materially to the welfare and development of mankind, should seem to have floundered into the morass of misunderstanding and incompetence where we now find them.

What it seems to me is needed is the replacement of the concept of consultation—which has become practically and rightly a dirty word—by one of partnership. Consultation even at its best infers a willingness of the decisive party to listen to the plea of the affected party. It has no connotation of joint debate of all the factors to reach the optimum in decision. There is something of the spider-and-fly encounter implicit in Government/industry consultation, even when carried out with all the niceties of administrative consideration. It is a process that risks making enemies rather than friends.

Of course, the concept of partnership is a difficult one for both sides. For Government it means coming out from behind the convenient shibboleths of parliamentary respect and fiscal confidence. It involves settling down to discussion with all the facts on the table—not just those of the suppliant. It means—much as with a board of directors—that, while the power of decision must not be shared, it must not either be abused by conclusions reached in despite of the balance of reason. These are hard concessions for Government, but necessary ones if its new initiative in the field of itself promoting prosperity is to succeed. On the industrial side there are entrenched positions which will need to be voluntarily surrendered as well. If the formula is partnership, then maximum disclosure must be exacted from industry no less than Government. Moreover, the right to make decisions with consideration solely for the individual enterprise can hardly be sustained. How, too, can one resist the right of Government to be selective and even discriminatory in its actions if those actions are the product of genuine and open debate between partners in the achievement of national prosperity?

Of course, there are the siren voices from both sides that must be resisted. There are those of Government who will see contamination only in such a partnership and the adulteration of pure social purposes in the cauldron of industrial chicanery. There will be those, too, on the industrial side who will maintain that the accumulation of the maximum effort of individuals acting autonomously for their own benefit equates with national prosperity and that any interference with that autonomy constitutes a dislocation which must be damaging in effect. Surely both these are wrong. In the circumstances of our island striving, with small natural resources and a large and sophisticated population, to provide a high standard of life at home and a valid contribution to the needs and safeguards of the world abroad, there must be comprehension, co-ordination, and collaboration between the generators and the apportioners of our national resources. Perhaps nowhere so much as here is such a sense of partnership needed in view of the precariousness of our economic equilibrium; it is grave indeed to register that perhaps nowhere is it less evident.

Ideally the system of partnership would envisage joint consideration of all areas of Government and industrial action having a bearing upon resources. I speak of industrial action because such is my task, but in no way imply in so doing that equivalent joint consideration is unrequired in other fields—educational, medical, recreational, etc.—where similar interaction occurs and should be the subject of bilateral or unilateral consideration accordingly. Thus there should be permanent joint consideration:

1. Of manpower problems to optimize the use of this resource. The conditions affecting remuneration, availability, training, redundancy, unemployment, sickness, location, and so on should be the subject of permanent scrutiny, and the potential improvements possible

through changes in these conditions should be fully analysed. This would be a far cry indeed from the present concept of the National Joint Advisory Council to the Secretary of State for Employment and Productivity, whose most ardent admirer could scarcely claim for it that it does more than allow the discharge of excess steam.

2. Of raw-materials problems to examine needs and availability; to ensure adequate but not excessive stocks; to identify shortfalls and review alternative means of meeting them; to consider ways of achieving greater economies in supply.

3. Of taxation problems with a view to identifying the means by which the levying of funds for Government use or for re-apportionment shall be devised the least possible to frustrate the generation of resources, or, in other words, to minimize the disincentives inherent in taxation of all kinds.

4. Of international trading problems to keep under permanent review the balance of concession and advantage inherent in overseas engagements and to devise changes likely to improve resources.

5. Of public purchasing problems to improve procurement arrangements in all fields of Government purchase with a view to the best use being made of resources available on the one side and to using procurement policy as a stimulus to resource-building on the other.

6. Of industrial standards and testing problems to rationalize and improve existing systems and to provide most urgently the kind of far-reaching and well-balanced authority in this whole field capable of reviving worldwide respect for British standards, specifications, and testing procedures.

7. Of land-use problems to ensure, as we move deeper into the twentieth century, that we do not, for want of forethought, provide incompetently for the use of our relatively small land area with resultant waste of resources for the future.

8. Of legal problems as affecting industry to ensure that the right balance is struck between the protection of the people from the depredation of renegades and the

enablement of industry to pursue prosperity unfettered by exaggerated and frustrating limitations.

9. Of investment problems to facilitate the most orderly build-up of resource-creating investment and to identify the causes of dislocation in such developments and the remedies available.

I am sure I could carry on almost indefinitely citing areas in which joint consideration between Government, management, unions, and others on a partnership basis could better ensure the examination of alternative courses of action than do present systems. Naturally it will be said that much consultation already takes place in all these fields, but, at the risk of repeating myself, I emphasize that what exists now has little chance of achieving what surely must be the common objective—namely, the optimization of resources. Where the climate of discussion is one steeped in reticence on both sides there can be little chance of objective and creative debate. And reticence there will be while one side to the discussion is fearful of having his evidence used against him and the other is unprepared to reveal his for fear of sullying his political immunity or forfeiting his right of decision.

The system I envisage is one divorced from the heat of party political debate and sited in an area of realism to analyse alternative courses of action and conclude on the impact these may have on the enrichment generally of the nation. The party political force in exercising its right of decision can then select its policies in the reasonable assurance that their impact has been objectively gauged.

Nowhere is the distinction more clear than in the field of national economic planning. In my concept there is a joint activity involved in identifying the outcome of all the subsidiary processes of joint consideration. The national plan—segregated wholly from political allegiance—is developed as an aggregation of the alternative conclusions reached in discussions aimed at the optimization of resources. The plan does not point an unwavering finger at a single conclusion, but seeks to demonstrate the impact of alternative permutations. It offers scope for the politicians to pick and choose their course in the light of their social policies, but it will not allow them to do so without recognizing the agreed implication of their acceptance and their rejections.

The outline I have presented depicts a present aridity in the mechanism of relations between industry and Government and seeks to promote a very different approach to this vital problem. I have no doubt that I shall be charged with having skated too easily over the surface, with little concern for the solidity and foundations of the structure I seek to change. I am utterly unrepentant. I am a firm believer in the evolution rather than the overthrow of institutions, and what I have sought to portray seems to me a reasonable and logical evolution of our present institutions to enable them to play the part they should in a tantalizing, risky, but potentially rewarding future. I feel deeply that on our present course of consultation by condescension we are moving into a deterioration of relationships between Government and industry, and I am anxious to see it arrested.

Conversely I am convinced that given the right circumstances of partnership between Government and industry we can bring about an industrial miracle here of which we could all be proud.

5 | Employers' Responsibility

by MARTIN JUKES, Q.C.

Martin Jukes, born in 1909, was educated at Merchant Taylors'
School and St John's College, Oxford, and was called to the Bar in
1933.
He won the Blackstone Prize for Common Law and was appointed
Queen's Counsel in 1954. His work at the Bar included industrial
accidents, advising employers and unions on matters affecting
conditions of employment, and general cases of Contract and Tort.
He was formerly Leader of the South Eastern Circuit, a Judge of
the Court of Appeal of the Channel Islands, and a Member of the
Bar Council. He is a Master of the Bench of the Middle Temple.
Mr Jukes is on the Council of the Confederation of British Industry
and several of the committees: he is a member of the National
Joint Advisory Council, which is chaired by the Secretary of State
for Employment and Productivity, and is a Member of the Engineer-
ing Industry Training Board as well as sitting on several of its
committees.
He joined the Engineering Employers' Federation as Director-
General Designate at the beginning of 1965 and became Director-
General a year later.
During the last war he reached the rank of Lieutenant-Colonel in
the RASC, worked on supplies for the liberated areas of Europe,
and was mentioned in dispatches.

The concept of the responsibility of an employer has both
changed and developed over the centuries. It has had to change
because the structure of industry itself and our own social
system and beliefs have also changed.

Industry as we know it today did not exist in the Middle
Ages. The chief industry was agriculture, and it was not carried
on, in general, for profit; it was carried on to feed the producers
and to pay dues to feudal lords and the Church. The raising of
capital for business purposes was hampered by the belief that
to lend money on interest was usury, except, perhaps, in the
field of merchant shipping. Apart from agriculture goods were
produced by artificers, who often had the raw material given
them; they were merely paid for their services. The attitude

was in general a paternal one; thus the apprentice to a trade normally lived with his master; equally, where a skilled man employed an assistant, the assistant was often regarded as part of the family. Wages were fixed under the Statute of Labourers by the Justices of the Peace. Part at least of the reason for this was the shortage of agricultural labour caused by the Black Death.

With the discovery that production could be increased by the division of labour, in that parts of an article were made by different men, modern industry began to develop into a form nearer that which we know today.

This development of industry led to an examination by early economists of the structure of industry and the philosophy that underlay the relations between master and man and buyer and seller.

One of the earliest and most famous of these economists was Adam Smith. In his *Wealth of Nations* he sought to analyse the working of the economy and the motives and beliefs that underlay it. His conclusion was that the two main principles were, first, self-interest and, second, natural liberty. He said: "It is not from the benevolence of the butcher, the brewer or the baker that we expect our dinner, but from their regard of their own interest. We address ourselves not to their humanity, but to their self-love, and never talk to them of our own necessities, but of their advantage."

The logical application of these principles led to conditions in industry in the eighteenth and early nineteenth centuries which we can only regard as wholly deplorable.

In *The Wealth of Nations* there is nothing of social justice and nothing of moral standards. In another famous passage Adam Smith says: "Every man so long as he does not violate the laws of justice is left perfectly free to pursue his own interests in his own way and to bring both his industry and his capital into competition with those of any other man or order of men." Carried to its logical conclusion, this would justify the employment of children in mines.

Yet Adam Smith's two principles have a great deal of truth in them today. Every incentive scheme used in industry is an appeal to a man's self-interest. The hostile reaction of both employers and unions to Government interference in industrial relations is an expansion of a desire to preserve natural liberty.

The views of Adam Smith came at a time when the Industrial Revolution was beginning. Crompton's mule was patented the year when *The Wealth of Nations* was published. Eleven years before Watt discovered the use of steam as a means of motion and power. These views were an expression of what men believed, and in particular employers believed, at that time.

The capitalist society which succeeded the feudal society was free from the restraints which modern society today places on it in the interests of society, of the community, and of men as individual human beings. There are some who condemn capitalism as such. Yet those who support it and regard free and private enterprise as an essential to free men would today accept restrictions imposed for the benefit of society. They accept such restrictions without question and often without thinking about them. Such restrictions are part of our life and social structure.

Our early industrial society was characterized by the mainspring of self-interest. Anything which interfered with the individual liberty of those who ran industry was opposed as a matter of principle. The views of Adam Smith were reinforced in the middle of the nineteenth century by Bentham, who, in *The Psychology of Economic Man*, wrote:

> That principle of action is most to be depended upon whose influence is most powerful, most constant and most uniform, most lasting and most general among mankind. Personal interest is that principle, a system of economy built on any other foundation is built on a quicksand.

Morality and ethics in general played no part in the relations between masters and men, and none in relation to the consumer and public interest.

Then and today it is essential to run a business at a profit, but the old beliefs led to the concentration of wealth in a few hands and great greed. Competition was unlimited. The law of supply and demand was seen as the most potent of all laws. It governed labour relations. If men could be got to work for semi-starvation wages it was legitimate to pay them semi-starvation wages; it was better, after all, to be half starved than to be completely starved and to die.

The relationship of master and man was based on the view that there was a contract between two free individuals striking a bargain about the price of the labour which the man would offer. Any interference with them was regarded as an interference with natural liberty. The bargain, of course, was one-sided in the extreme. All the economic power lay on the side of the master. The man was under compulsion to sell his labour. If he did not others would like his place. If he displeased his master it might be that no other employer would take him on. Early efforts by workmen to combine were regarded by masters as a wicked conspiracy. Severe sentences were passed on those who joined in early attempts at combination. One only has to look at the case of the Tolpuddle Martyrs to see this. Yet these sentences reflected the social beliefs of many at that time.

The economic weakness of the working-man was accentuated by a number of other factors. Most of them had little if any education, and many could not read. Labour was in general not skilled. It was an age of growing mass-production based on unskilled labour.

The picture of industry during the half-century or so after the start of the Industrial Revolution from the social point of view was an unhappy one. It was the age of the industrialist who owned his own business. His responsibility was in the main to himself and to no-one else.

There were, of course, exceptions to this unhappy picture. Men like Owen reacted against the industrial philosophy of their time. Gradually social consciousness awoke and protested against the conditions of industry and the exploitation of men, women, and children. Parliament itself expressed this growing social consciousness by passing Acts to give some measure of protection to the safety and health of workers in factories and mines, and regulated the employment of women and children. But for a long time there was a clash between the humanitarians and those whose philosophy was that of Bentham. Even with the latter one found many who were kind and compassionate to individuals and sincere Christians, yet whose treatment of their workpeople was conditioned by the principles of Bentham, that personal interest was the only foundation for the conduct of industry.

There came also a greater toleration of unions. It was realized by more and more people that men had a right to combine together to secure and protect their standards of living. Unions were given some protection in the second half of the nineteenth century by statute. Further, after the courts in 1904 whittled down the protection which up till then they had enjoyed the Trades Disputes Act of 1906 was passed to restore their protection. It is interesting to note that this Act adopted the views of a minority of the Royal Commission which sat to consider their rights. The majority were not in favour of restoring them.

There were, of course, many other factors at work. The social structure was changing. Views about the position of the individual in society were developing. Karl Marx produced *Das Kapital*. Educational opportunities for working-men were growing. The majority were no longer illiterate. The attack on individual wealth was carried on by Lloyd George. The whole attitude of the employer to his workers was challenged, and by the early part of this century the rights of the employee were the subject of a growing recognition by ordinary men and by the State.

Even wages were the subject of State intervention where workers were not adequately represented by unions. Minimum wages were established by wages boards.

In general the unions grew in strength. Their strength provoked the creation of a counterweight—namely, the employers' associations. The struggle here was to preserve the management's right to manage and to prevent encroachments on their rights by unions. It led to many bitter struggles, of which one of the last major ones was in 1922 in the engineering industry.

But perhaps the greatest change in the whole philosophy of management's responsibilities has come in the years after the end of the Second World War.

Until the Second World War it was still possible to believe that within the framework of duties imposed by statute the employer's responsibility was solely to himself or his shareholders. It is not possible now.

The area of the duties which the employer owes to his employee has been immensely widened by statutory intervention. The concept of the duty a manufacturer or seller owes to the public, and also to the general welfare and economic health of the nation, is now recognized.

Industry itself has changed at the same time. Businesses are now rarely privately owned. They are for the most part managed by professional managers. The attitude of the professional manager must inevitably be different from that of the owner-manager. Companies are growing in size. In some sections of industry only the largest have the resources to finance the research and development and overseas marketing which are needed to survive. But growth in size in itself creates its own problems in industrial relations. Top management becomes more and more remote from the employee on the shop floor. The recognition of these problems has created the need for a new kind of person, the personnel director or manager. He is quite a different person from the labour manager, whom he sometimes succeeded and whose main function was the supply of labour. The personnel director requires new knowledge and new skills in industrial relations.

Both unions and employers' associations have also changed in their outlook and in their view of their responsibilities. Unions were formed to protect their members and raise their standard of life. Employers' associations were at first purely defensive, and existed to protect their members from the demands of the unions, and in particular from any attempt to interfere in the employer's right to manage. Today there is a recognition of mutual interests. There is a much broader view of their responsibilities. Both sides recognize the paramount need to keep industry prosperous and the need to co-operate on many issues. The very fact that the TUC on its own can have an incomes policy which is intended to act as a restraint upon its member unions in the demands they make for increases in wages would have been quite inconceivable fifty years ago, and barely conceivable before the Second World War. Trade unions and employers sit upon the "little Neddies" together, seeking to improve the productivity and prosperity of their particular industry. They also sit on bodies such as training boards, where a remarkable degree of agreement is frequently obtained.

Employers have long passed from the idea of unrestrained natural liberty. A very large proportion of them belong to employers' associations in which they agree to voluntary restraints upon their own freedom of action. They now accept as natural, responsibilities which thirty years ago would have been inconceivable.

The concept of the employers' responsibility has thus gradually developed and transformed itself, so that instead of Adam Smith's two principles of self-interest and natural liberty there is now acceptance of responsibility to shareholders, to the enterprise itself, to the employees, to the customers of the enterprise, and to the public and the State. Industry must make a profit or perish, but its existence is important socially.

There are very few companies which are today privately controlled, and even fewer that are privately owned. Death duties and the constant necessity to raise fresh capital will make these numbers ever smaller. So the employer now is in general the professional manager, and the owners of the business are the shareholders. The manager is using their capital in the business, which they have invested in to get their reward.

Many would still put as the first of the employer's responsibilities his duty to his shareholders. Unless things go badly wrong, shareholders often are in no position to judge and have no knowledge of whether their interests are being properly looked after. They are bound to take on trust much of what is done for them, yet they may be neglected at the manager's peril. Shareholders who do not get their proper reward by way of dividends and some appreciation of the share price may not wish to invest further in the company and provide the further capital which may be needed in the future.

Closely akin to the responsibility of the employer, who today is the professional manager, is the duty to the enterprise itself. Its basic duty is to be efficient and stay in existence. This involves not only the proper and economic handling of the enterprise but adaptation to change and technological advance. There may, of course, be other economic results, such as the benefit to the community by the production of some commodity. But basically the responsibility is to produce a commodity which is required at a price the consumer is prepared to pay. In a country like England, which must export to live, manufacturers must also produce what the foreign buyer requires at a price he will pay. Indeed, the responsibility to the community may require that goods should be sold abroad at a less profit than can be obtained in the home market.

The employer accordingly is responsible that his organization is adequate; that his staff is of the right quality and properly trained; that he can keep up with his competitors abroad as well as at home in his research and his adaptation to modern technology. These particular responsibilities have also evolved. Promotion now is more upon merit and personal ability than family connection. The need for management-training is now being more fully recognized. Management has many skills, and though some who have risen to the top of industry have acquired these without formal training, there is a great and growing need for training among potential managers.

It is perhaps in the area of responsibility towards employees that the responsibility of the employer has been enlarged most. It is in this area that most of the statutory duties have been imposed upon employers. In particular there has come in the last twenty years the concept that an employee is much more than a man who sells his labour to an employer, and who can be dispensed with at will or when his labour is no longer required. The concept seems to be that the employee is part of the company; that he contributes to it in the same way as the shareholder contributes his capital. The concept is a socialist as opposed to a capitalist one. But it seems to have come to stay, as it is unlikely that a Conservative Government would repeal the Redundancy Payments Act which enshrines it. It establishes a proprietary right in a job after a certain time. The proprietary right becomes more valuable as service with the company increases. A man who loses his job because there is no work for him to do is thus entitled to compensation.

It is now urged that this proprietary right, recognized by the Redundancy Payments Act, should be further strengthened by permitting anyone dismissed to appeal to some outside body, unless he is dismissed for redundancy—*i.e.*, there is no work for him to do. Thus an extension of the employer's responsibility is sought—namely, that he may not dismiss an employee except for redundancy without grounds that will stand examination in an industrial court.

At present most industries have procedures for settling disputes. There are generally committees of employers and union officials. Dismissal cases, of course, come within the scope of such procedures. Experience would seem to show that compromises are often reached with dismissal cases in procedure, and the employee is taken back. It is doubtful whether many such results would come out of an industrial tribunal, where the atmosphere would be one of legal justification rather than the wider human approach. In any court our present law provides that no-one can be forced to work for a particular employer, and no employer can be forced to employ a particular worker.

Presumably no industrial tribunal could require an employee to be taken back into an employer's employment but would only award compensation.

Important though a man's right to his job may be, it is perhaps of even greater importance that he should work as a reasonably contented member of a team. He is not just a hired hand; he is a human being with all of a human being's need for satisfaction in his job and a knowledge of what the enterprise of which he is part is doing. Many modern writers have drawn attention to this. High on the list of those things which are essential to the smooth running and efficiency of an enterprise is good communication with workers on the shop floor.

Employees, particularly those on the shop floor, are generally conservative and resistant to change. So are many employers. They tend to view new methods of work or payment, the introduction of new machines, a system of work study and job evaluation with suspicion. Only good communications which provide the explanation for what is being done and the reason for it can remove the suspicions. Indeed, a great deal of discontent and industrial action, whether by strike or go-slow, can be attributed to insufficient communication.

But close to the responsibility of the employer for letting his employees know in general what the business is trying to do, and why it is doing it, comes the duty of consultation with employees. Of course, it is the duty and responsibility of the employer to manage. The employer has usually the knowledge of what is possible and desirable. He alone can judge the financial implication, the possible sources of supply of materials and markets available, for instance. He alone must be responsible for designing the product so that it may meet the needs of the potential market. But while there are large areas of management decisions in which consultation with employees would be valuable to both sides, there are also substantial areas where a lack of consultation would be not only unwise but also fatal to normal working.

The re-equipment of a factory with up-to-date machines or the installation of numerical control which will permit more than one machine to be worked by a single operator is clearly a management responsibility. But it may create the problem of displacement of labour. Not so many operators are required as before, or a less skilled worker can now, by use of modern machinery, do work which previously required a skilled man. Where changes such as these are made not only an explanation of them—*i.e.*, communication—is necessary, but also consultation. Such consultation can only be with the representatives of the men initially. Shop stewards are such representatives, and without them consultation and communication would be very difficult, if not impossible.

Another area where communication and consultation are essential if success is to be achieved is the introduction of work study and job evaluation, both of which are desirable in themselves and are also the basic necessities of a productivity bargain. Work study in general involves the timing of operations. Such timing is generally regarded with the greatest suspicion. It is thought that an endeavour is being made to get much more work out of a man without any further payment. Of course, this is not true. The object of work study, as well as job evaluation, is to see that production is more efficient. It helps to show where delays and bottlenecks occur so that they may be remedied. Another fear of work study is that it leads to redundancies. This is not necessarily so, but if it does the long-term interests of the firm and its employees must be explained. Memories of the bad times in the thirties before the War still linger.

Indeed, in cases such as this, it is not only necessary to explain what is going to be done but also to get agreement about it. The duty and responsibility of management to manage still remain. It is still their responsibility to ensure maximum efficiency, but the willingness of their work force to co-operate is a condition of the achievement of efficiency.

Yet another aspect of the employer's responsibility to his employees is the movement to put worker-directors on to the board of a company. This is proposed in the nationalized steel industry. In Germany there are worker-directors on the supervisory board of a company in the steel industry. This board is non-executive, as there is in addition an executive board which is subject to the policy directions of the supervisory board. In France there is a somewhat similar provision for worker-directors, but their duties appear to be really those of observers. It does not appear that these worker-directors have added much to the efficiency of industry in Germany or France. It is also doubtful whether industrial relations have been improved by their presence.

In Great Britain the idea of worker-directors on the boards of the nationalized steel industry has not been enthusiastically received by all the trade unions. Indeed, one powerful union, the Electrical Trades Union, has declared its opposition to it. A worker representative may not have the ability or the knowledge to make a useful contribution to the proceedings of the board. Further, his very presence on the board and his association with its decisions may handicap trade-union activities and be an actual embarrassment where wages questions are involved.

The employer's responsibilities to his employees do not, of course, consist merely in cultivating good industrial relations; they go farther. Safety and training are two other major responsibilities. Accidents provide a greater loss of man hours than strikes, but they are not always so damaging to production. Illness or injury to one or more men rarely closes a department down; a strike frequently does. But the problem of accidents and industrial disease is a serious one. The figures of those injured in industry have continued to grow each year. Part of their increase is probably due to better reporting of accidents, but not all the increase. Further, the majority of industrial accidents are preventable, and in a very large number of cases are due to ignorance or negligence. This is a matter to which a good deal of thought is being given by industry, and in particular management, at the moment. Management would accept probably that the primary responsibility lies on it. It is for management to instil into workers the need for safety, the care that is needed to avoid injury to others, and the way in which injury may be caused. But perhaps the most important aspect is the need for close supervision, with safety in mind. Safety officers are invaluable when a firm is large enough to employ them, but shop-floor supervision is probably the most important factor.

The responsibility for training is now made of considerable importance by the Training Act. It was always important, but some firms did very little training and secured their skilled men from other firms. Since in a technological age industry must provide skills if it is to survive, training for these skills on an industrial basis is essential. This is one of the objects of the Training Act and the boards set up under it. Another object is to set standards of training which will be uniform, and to see that the best methods of training are adopted.

Finally one must consider the responsibility which an employer owes to the public and to the national interest. He has responsibilities as such to society. This is a concept recognized by legislation covering a wide field. Both the Monopolies Commission and the Prices and Incomes Board exist to guard the public interest. Companies may be told that their profits are excessive, or that they may not increase their prices. They may even be told that their advertising expenditure is too great and that it should be reduced so that the price of the product may be reduced to the consumer. Leaving aside Acts of Parliament which deal with the quality of the goods sold, such as the Food and Drugs Act, the duty to the consumer seems now accepted. However, the duties which an Incomes Policy seeks to establish are by no means accepted by employer and employee. Yet, whichever view is right on that issue, the principles of self-interest and individual liberty which were Adam Smith's guiding light have been modified and limited to a stage where Adam Smith would not recognize them. Many today have serious doubts whether the present degree of Government interference in industry is not a hindrance to efficiency.

6 | *Some Human Values of the Manager*

by JOHN MARSH

Since the war John Marsh has been successively director of the Institute of Personnel Management, the Industrial (Welfare) Society, and since 1961 Director-General of the British Institute of Management. Originally a production engineer in the motor industry, he was profoundly influenced by his war experience as an army major at Dunkirk and Singapore and later as a camp-commander prisoner of war on the notorious Burma-Siam Railway. John Marsh has wide interests, and his 'extramural' activities have included the original idea and administration of H.R.H. the Duke of Edinburgh's Study Conference of 1956, the first Chairmanship of Voluntary Service Overseas, Chairman of the British National Conference on Social Work 1957–59, and membership of Government Enquiries into the Youth Service and Work in Prisons. He has travelled, studied, and lectured extensively in twenty-six countries in the field of management and human relations. The author of three books of essays, he married actress Mary Costerton in 1950 and has four children.

"Do you wish to be the wealthiest business manager ever cremated at Golders Green?" This is a question I sometimes fling at managerial audiences when we are discussing the manager and his need for a personal philosophy. Does his happiness match his wealth, does his purpose in life achieve fulfilment? This we'll never know, but it might be worth making an assessment of some of the values involved in answering this question.

The modern managerial job is a tough one if it is to be effective in getting results in an increasingly competitive and complex age. I would define a manager as someone who is concerned with the proper, systematic, and profitable use of resources under his control. In this sense modern management attitudes, policies, and practices need to be more widely applied in all sectors of a mixed economy, certainly in Government and local government and in the social services—as well as in all forms of competitive enterprise. Management is concerned with

74

growth—whereas administration is usually concerned with keeping things going. Management involves decision-making and risk-taking. We now know that knowledge of management can be learned almost continuously throughout a managerial career—knowledge plus experience and tested personal qualities form the alchemy of managerial success.

Management is a combination of art and science—the science lies in the areas which can be quantified by measurement and results. The art lies in getting things done through people—by far the most difficult yet rewarding part of the manager's job.

We all have views on this, and psychologists and sociologists are increasingly committing themselves to print about the motivation of managers—as individuals and in groups. Many of these cases, findings, and emerging theories in the behavioural sciences are bewildering in their jargon and meaning, and for older managers even more unintelligible than chapters in the Old Testament when considered in relation to the hurly-burly of business relationships. Nevertheless these researches have relevance for those who can study the use of people in the tactical exercises arising out of business case studies. I would perhaps betray age more than cynicism in stating that tomorrow's manager is in peril both in ignoring and in using the 'know-how' of the behavioural sciences.

Just after the war Professor Elton Mayo—it is too often forgotten that he was an Australian—had a remarkable world-wide influence with his Hawthorne Studies; his expensive but simple findings underlined some of the values we need to remember when dealing with the individual and the group at work. Seebohm Rowntree in a series of what I would call 'hardware' studies reminded us of the economics of compassion. Their successors are less direct in their messages—but we must persevere in trying to understand them.

There is a wealth of good and bad example in the experience of our managerial predecessors—and in most of us. There is a sad absence of readable and human biographies of British industrialists and management pioneers—of whom there have been a large number. Publishers would render a distinctive service to the future of competitive enterprise in Britain if they should quickly decide to commission a series of such biographies, but the stories must be realistic and stress the humanity of these men—warts and all.

Example and Discipleship

Each of us learns a good deal in our early experience of being 'managed' by others. To the young employee 'the boss' has above all the air of authority; he seems in control (whether he is or not—we learn later!), and his words, virtues, and frailties are the common currency of groups in all workplaces.

Some of my earlier memories of managerial wisdom include the following:

> Always arrive five minutes early for an appointment; lateness is disrespect to the other person—even if he is a junior.
> Some blokes teach more effectively by a drop of silence than others do in a bucket of words. (Foreman when placing me under the control of a taciturn chargehand.)
> I may be responsible for the production of 100,000 cars a year—this is a grand result—but my biggest responsibility lies in the well-being of 20,000 workers who help to make them; I can never really know if I succeed in my leadership of men—leadership is your capacity for influencing others so that they willingly do their work well. (The late John Hannay, Production Manager, Austin Motor Co., Ltd.)
> Every man has an example in him somewhere for you—a lesson of what to do and what not to do—therefore be grateful to him for it.
> You may not think much of him at work, but he is a fine husband and father, and this is what life is all about.

All of us are the disciples of others, and such is the human tradition that we soon in our turn are the conscious rather than the unwitting exemplars of others. The experience and wisdom of one generation tends to be overridden when another takes over, but real values and example come surging back on the tide of human progress. In this sense all of us have the chance to be leaders and begetters of leaders—especially if we create disciples in our heyday, not in our decline. I am convinced that through this process the 'divine spark' is kindled in others, and its continuity, the 'good character' of a business (or a department of a business) is ensured. You cannot legislate for this in glossy personnel policies.

Power and its Influence

To manage people, events, or processes in the achievement of results means the exercise of power. The power to get things done can be a heady experience for all of us at times—and it takes time for judgment to modify enthusiasm in exercising it. The manager needs continually to study power—its essence and its influence on himself and others. Its essence means the personal assumption of final responsibility for the task we have been set, and we know with the authority of power there is the concomitant responsibility of 'carrying the can'. Many a good functional man has been ruined by being unprepared for the assumption of power over others, and even more by the struggle of power politics—the ruthless determination of his contemporaries with similar powers to win the day in work situations. Let us admit at once that power politics amongst ambitious people is no new phenomenon—it happens in women's institutes, football clubs, trade unions, and most certainly in ecclesiastical circles. I remember the reassurance of reading that the famous Dean Inge had not spoken to a certain cleric in St Paul's Cathedral over many years!

The complex organization of business, with its departmentalism, its urgencies, its alternative courses of action, all means that there is room for bidding in priorities, for allocations, and for early or later success. In this setting the clash of personalities is part of the conflict of ideas and opinions, and winning the support of the Managing Director is not only a functional triumph, but often a blue-eyed-boy achievement too—at least in the view of those who are unsuccessful.

And yet—as Sir Frederick Hooper wisely put it some years ago—it is a question ultimately of power *with* people rather than over people. There are men who will never know the difference—and I would guess that they have their moments of desperate uneasiness.

In my view there is everything to be said for vitality and healthy competitiveness in the power-political relationships of equals—but it is very much a matter for the co-ordinating manager to watch the balance of these forces with good humour and to make sure that it all adds up to teamwork in achieving the end result.

The Art of being a Colleague

Counterbalancing power politics is the art of colleagueship. Most of us know the time taken up in committee, group, or unilateral discussions. Very few decisions are made by one man;

most are reached out of a consensus of view, based on a review of facts and a careful weighing of probabilities, in which the give and take of opposing views requires disciplined discussion and listening. Once decisions are made, each takes away his task and has final responsibility for his part in achieving a corporate result.

I have known managers with remarkable chips on their shoulders because they had been passed over for promotion to the boards of their companies, and no-one was able to tell them the real truth; in most cases they were not considered capable of being congenial colleagues; they had strong but narrow expertise and views—they were intolerant of criticism, and, in short, as people they were bores. The art of being a colleague demands that we should respect the expertise, experience, and qualities of others, that we should be capable of open-mindedness about broad issues, be objective in weighing up the potential of junior staff, and be generous in encouraging them to become our peers or betters. With our sons we have no doubts on this score! Above all, our loyalty should be manifest to our colleagues, not clouded by jealousies. The family business is perhaps more prone to desperate situations in this respect.

Work, Marriage, and Home Life

For every manager, ambition and the pursuit of excellence in his job is a healthy approach to successful achievement. I hardly know a happy manager, however, who does not have continually to face up to the question of the correct balance between his marriage and home life and his work. There is too often a deep conflict between the demands of work and the calls of home. Of course, this problem has many parallels in other professional groups. Many professional tasks are more solitary, such as those in medical general practice and the law; even there the patient or client may cause extraordinary intrusion on home life, but it could be argued that the wife knew what she was taking on. In the case of the manager, in his early days of work and marriage he is somewhat sheltered from the demands of corporate managerial activity—the larger the firm, the more crucial and the more open-ended this kind of involvement.

It requires a very frank relationship between the manager and his wife for each to be content with the often impersonal needs of the work situation—drawing heavily on the sacrifice of both partners in marriage. It is argued that behind every successful man is a wife of great patience, tolerance, and understanding; it is easy to say this, but marriage as the richest of human relationships has the added concern of children, and the process of bringing them up demands the manifest love of both parents.

In gentler days (were there ever any in terms of human conflict or passion?) the busy man and his wife of the middle classes could subcontract some of their responsibilities to the boarding-school system. In this age of massive nuclear threat, and the greater immediacy of the world, national, and local problems, purveyed to us constantly by the media of television, radio, and Press, it is questionable whether such subcontracting is at all adequate. If children cannot really establish a *rapport* with their busy parents, in particular with the preoccupied businessman father, then one wonders if we have our human priorities in the right order. In advanced industrial countries where severe changes in customs and values are accelerating there are disturbing signs of cynicism and protest in the children, who at base react against the system of society which deprives them of some irreplaceable human essentials. I think there is a strong and urgent case for a great understanding by employers of these problems and the stress they cause to key employees and their wives. Very often a manager opts out of the rat-race with no intention whatever of being less efficient at the level he has attained, but because he has reached a vital human decision in his work and family relationships. In advanced countries with acute labour shortages we see almost for the first time in history a large élite class who have no time to relax at home in what used to be termed 'gracious living'—for at home the responsible husband and his equally responsible wife have endless household and social chores to perform, which may indeed be distraction, but scarcely genuine relaxation and refreshment.

Paradoxically, millions of the managers' fellow-workers find work less intellectually or physically demanding—though not in frustration—but they can with certainty give real time to family and leisure pursuits. Who, indeed, is the more fortunate at the end of the day—the more ambitious, the potentially wealthier treadmill manager—or he who is more the master of his own spare time? Whose is the real achievement in terms of human success; who might gain the whole world and yet lose his own soul? In this area of achieving human fulfilment lies the unknown but certain judgment of our heirs.

Know Thyself

In managing we have but a short spell in which to achieve excellence; our creative years are brief; our many acquaintanceships and few friendships at work can constitute the sum of our contribution to human values in that situation; our expectations of ourselves and subordinates need to be exacting if our business is to survive and be profitable; we shall have occasions requiring courage to dismiss employees for inefficiency or human incompatibility; after the painful decision to dispense with a man's services we need at once to be compassionate in helping him to find his new level in the rough market-place of further employment—"there but for the grace of God go I". All men have common frailties—our differences lie in concealing them. To those who share success we must be as proportionately generous as we ourselves hope to be treated. As time goes on we inevitably become more obsolescent, and it will require a magnanimous philosophy to make way for the young who in a later age echo our own early impatience. As retirement nears we need still to be open to the encouragement of change in the belief that on the foundation of our modest achievements others will build more strongly, with greater effect in a world constantly demanding more in results.

And as for the rest—as husbands, as fathers, as citizens, as friends—as members of a fascinating, restless, constantly surprising society, we have love to give and take, duties to render, debts to pay, loyalties to win and retain in our striving and search for values and fulfilment.

7 | Management Education and Values

by MICHAEL P. FOGARTY

Professor Michael Fogarty was born in 1916. He was a Fellow of Nuffield College from 1944 to 1951 and Professor of Industrial Relations, University College, Cardiff, from 1951 to 1966. At present he is a Consultant with Political and Economic Planning. He has also worked for the Oxford Institute of Statistics, the National Institute of Economic and Social Research, *The Economist*, and the Ministry of Town and Country Planning. He is the author of a number of books, including:

> *The Just Wage;*
> *The Rules of Work;*
> *Company and Corporation—One Law?*
> PEP Broadsheets: *Wider Business Objectives;*
> *Companies beyond Jenkins;*
> *A Companies Act 1970?*

Business values are an important part of our culture, and their study is an important part of general or 'liberal' education. Management education, however, is first and foremost vocational, and the inclusion in it of the study of values has to be justified by a practical need. The practical need arises because, in the changing and complex conditions of modern economies, those who direct businesses have found it increasingly necessary to be explicit about the purposes which their businesses are to serve and the way in which priorities between these purposes are established.

A business depends for its survival on a mutually profitable exchange of services with a number of interests both inside and outside it, including its suppliers of finance, labour, and plant and raw materials, its customers, related businesses, and the national and local communities in which it operates. Its success in this exchange is likely to be measured in terms both of its relations to individual interests and of the overall image which it projects as a result of these relations. A number of these interests have become increasingly effective in recent years in expressing what they want from business and in insisting that business shall give it to them. The power and readiness of the State to intervene in business has increased immensely. Employees have been able to exert more power, not only through unions or political action, but as a result of full employment and of the rising proportion of employees with high technical and managerial qualifications whose views a firm cannot afford to overlook. Customers have become increasingly able to bring the law or publicity to their help. Competition in consumer markets has become tougher as a result of new possibilities of finding substitutes for existing products, of new methods of distribution, and of the greater flexibility of consumers' expenditure with the rise of income and smaller commitment of it to fixed basic needs. Businesses are increasingly expected not merely to meet established, competitive standards of service to these various interests but to keep these standards steadily advancing. Small firms with limited markets and influence may be able to get by with a good level of performance in one or two respects and a modest minimum in others. Larger firms are expected to achieve high and rising standards all round.

It is not merely a question of expecting businesses, while giving their main attention to one or two objectives such as customer service and profit, also to bear in mind more marginal objectives in areas such as relations with the Government, local communities, or employees. The significance of the decisions which firms are today expected to take in areas like these is often from the firm's point of view anything but marginal. The commitment of resources which they involve can be massive. A firm has no more valuable resource than the time of its top executives; and the National Industrial Conference Board have found that it is common in large American firms for chief executives to spend upwards of 40 per cent of their time "in dealing with environmental problems of governmental, civic and community relations; philanthropy; and education generally". Decisions about location and amenities in which firms are expected to pay attention to the needs of local communities may have fundamental consequences for a firm's whole future. Even minor adjustments in employee conditions may have a greatly magnified impact on the margin of profit or loss.

Nor is a firm's choice of how best to look after the various interests which impinge on it simply a matter of a conditioned response, of finding the one right answer. There rarely if ever is one right answer. Firms can achieve the financial results which allow them to survive in a number of different ways. Within quite wide limits they can choose for themselves whether they do, or do not, wish to build themselves a reputation for advanced personnel practice or active involvement in community relations or as leaders in relatively basic types of research, or whether they wish to be known as loyal members of their industrial association or to go it alone. Business executives must today have not only very great power but a very great area of discretion if they are to do what the public expects of them. Not only do their decisions have a major impact on economic growth, on patterns of consumption, on social relations, on the physical appearance of communities, or on the distribution of population and today even on international relations, if they are to get results in a changing and difficult environment, they have to have a relatively free hand in these decisions. They must certainly be accountable for the purposes for which they use the power this gives them. If, however, control and accountability were to cut into their freedom of action to an extent which interfered seriously with results, the public would prefer to cut the controls and get the results. Businessmen cannot expect others to define their priorities and strategies for them. They have to define them, in large part, for themselves.

Nor, finally, in the modern world can businessmen escape the need to make their priorities and strategies explicit. In simpler, more slowly changing economies the relation of a business to its environment and to the various groups within the business itself may be defined perfectly satisfactorily by custom and practice. But once change and complexity and the scale and diversity of operations develop in the way familiar in large and advanced businesses today, reliance on policies defined only by custom and experience quickly leads to confusion and mismanagement. A few years ago the trial on anti-trust charges of a number of senior executives of American electrical machinery firms brought sharply home to American industry that boards of directors are often not fully aware of the policies being carried out lower down in their business or in control of them. One of the recent trends documented by the National

Industrial Conference Board has accordingly been for American firms to make their internal definitions of policy sharper and more explicit, not in order to tie subordinates down or deprive them of their proper discretion, but in order to provide enough guide-lines to ensure that their actions form part of a coherent and considered whole.

These are the very practical reasons from the side of business experience which have led in recent years to increasing interest in including in management education the study of business values and how best to balance one purpose against another. A further factor from the side of management education itself has been the shift of emphasis in the leading business schools from how-to-do-it techniques to training students in the way to identify and choose between new policies and methods for the future. Business schools must, of course, be concerned to some extent with passing on established techniques and practice. More and more, however, their value to business has been seen to lie not so much in teaching how things are done now as in producing managers and professional men who can think two steps ahead of the present situation, identify problems not yet clearly visible, and force the pace towards the techniques and strategies most appropriate for solving them. If decision-making in this wider and longer-term sense is to be at the centre of business studies, these studies must necessarily include the analysis of values. The end product of managerial decision-making is a judgment that this or that *ought* to be done, and the value premises behind the judgment are as much part of the decision process as the premises of fact. A business school which concentrates on how-to-do-it can afford to ignore this, since its problem is not to decide which ends to pursue, but to develop students' capacity to use the available means to reach a given set of ends. But for a school which focuses on the selection of new objectives the study of values is compulsory.

What then is to be taught under this head, and what is the best approach to teaching it?

WHAT IS TO BE TAUGHT?

(a) Case Skills

Some businessmen are by common consent outstanding for their ability to make sound judgments based not only on profit but on principle. The first characteristic of such a man is that he has in a high degree skill in analysing and deciding cases. He knows how to identify the problems at the back of the case and the considerations they involve. He can balance these considerations impartially in the light of the relevant values and standards and arrive at solutions generally acceptable in the actual, concrete, and varying circumstances of each situation. He does not simply go by the book, nor does his understanding of values stop at broad general principles.

A number of firms and business organizations have tried to develop codes of business ethics. The American Management Association has published a collection of these codes—together with comments by the firms concerned—on the practical value which they have had. Codes which consist merely of broad affirmations of principle applicable at every time and place have proved to have little practical value. To write a code of this kind may be educative for those who take a direct and personal part in doing so; but otherwise this sort of code has little practical impact and is quickly forgotten. The codes which do have an impact are the ones which, like those developed by advertisers in Britain and America, come closely to grips with the actual situations currently faced by practitioners, and show in practical detail how the intricate balance of considerations which they involve can be sorted out. Ethics are a practical subject, not a field of theoretical analysis, and training in them for business or other purposes must focus above all on how to act in practical situations in the light of the differing circumstances of each one.

(b) Working Rules

However, effective case skills do not consist only in making snap decisions on such factors as are immediately obvious in a situation. They also consist in bringing to bear wider experience from related cases, analysed and reflected on more thoroughly than is usually possible in the rush of an immediate situation. This wider experience is embodied first of all in the practical rules which each individual discovers in his environment and develops for himself in areas of work where he has experience. Every job and firm and economy has, and must have, a set of working rules representing recognized good practice, and a man of good business judgment has to be familiar with these and to develop his own view and code of them.

Some of these rules are explicit and are written down in laws, rule books, or collective agreements. Others are a matter simply of informal understanding among practitioners. They cover every field of business practice. There are standards for advertising and labelling, for collective bargaining, for fairness in pay or in the relations between a purchasing officer and his firm's suppliers, or about the relation between a trade association and its members, or between financial institutions in the City. There are expectations about the degree of dynamism which a firm should show. Whereas once a firm could get by with observing relatively static, established, standards of pay or productivity, today it is likely to be looked at askance if it does not provide steadily rising standards for its employees and contribute by research and development to improving its own and the economy's ability to serve customers. A similar expectation of growth has come to be built into people's norms for the working of the economy as a whole. Other expectations have arisen about regional and international development. Twenty years ago, towards the end of the first phase of Development Area policy in Britain, it was possible to trace through the files of the Board of Trade and the records of development agencies the emergence of a whole series of new conventions about the contribution which firms could reasonably be asked to make towards solving regional development problems and the way in which their contribution could be best be encouraged or enforced. Today, as more and more corporations become involved in operations overseas and as international organizations develop and formerly backward peoples begin to stand up for their rights, a further body of assumptions is growing up about a firm's duties over international development.

The force of the conventions and expectations within which a firm operates varies greatly, and is not always visible on the face of any particular rule. It is not always the rules laid down by law which are the most important or the most strongly binding in practice. Some rules are tentative, still in process of formation and surrounded by a haze of uncertainty. Others are clear-cut but beginning to break up under the impact of new experience. It is part of sound business judgment to know not merely what rules exist but what is the current force of each, and what changes are likely within the length of time of which account has to be taken, and in which direction.

(c) Underlying Values and Attitudes

Behind these more specific working rules there lie more general values and attitudes. Some people are inclined to be radical, others conservative, some are more authoritarian and others more democratic, some tougher and others more tender-minded. Eduard Spranger developed a distinction between the theoretical man who is interested in the discovery of facts and the relations between them; the economic man who is interested in the practical affairs of the business world; the aesthetic man interested chiefly in form and harmony; the social man for whom the basic value is the love of people and whose outlook is altruistic and philanthropic; the political man whose interest is in power; and the religious man who seeks to relate himself to the ultimate values and forces of the universe. The mixture of values and attitudes like these in different personalities and the culture of different social or national groups has a very direct effect on practical action. A man of practical judgment needs to be aware of which attitudes are appropriate to which cases—when, for example, an authoritarian pattern of management is appropriate and when a democratic pattern—and what the values and attitudes held by himself and by those with whom he deals inside and outside his organization are, and how far and on what points they differ.

(d) Change and Conflict

There is, of course, often a clash between values, attitudes, and working rules as understood by different individuals and groups, and between the ways in which individuals or groups see rules and values to apply in different situations. Sometimes clashes of this sort are more apparent than real. A lawyer in court who puts the case for his client and does his best to demolish that of the other side is not following a different set of rules or values from his opponent or the judge. He is merely performing a different role within an overall framework of rules and conventions designed as a whole to ensure that justice is done. In the same way a sales manager, a personnel manager, a purchasing officer, or a public-relations officer will often have to act within his firm in some sense as the ambassador of customers, labour, suppliers, or the general public, reminding the firm of what a mutually satisfactory relationship with each of these groups implies and keeping it aware of the obligations this relationship imposes on it. The specialist who acts in this way is not in any fundamental sense in conflict with other specialists performing a similar role in relation to other groups, though he may, of course, differ from them on particular policies. He is simply performing one specialist role within the total pattern of roles by which his organization's purposes are defined and achieved.

Sometimes a clash is genuine but arises from misunderstandings rather than from underlying reality. A very common finding is that people of one class, or in one function, perceive people in other classes and functions as holding opinions much more different from their own and much more hostile to them than is actually the case. Supervisors' and shop stewards' attitudes to each other tend to be distorted in this way. So do the mutual attitudes of executives and scientists; and of men and women. A significant factor in women's failure to reach top jobs has been that though men's and women's perceptions of ideal masculine and feminine behaviour are actually very much the same, men see women as trying to push them into behaving in a much less masculine way and women see men as trying to push them into behaving in a much more feminine way than either sex actually intends. Misunderstandings of this sort are often deeply ingrained and hard to remove.

To them have to be added clashes which arise not from misunderstanding, but from genuine differences of view. Widely differing opinions are obviously held on questions such as the case for limiting advertising expenditure, or how to design a wage and price policy which will meet the needs of national policy on inflation and the balance of payments as well as those of individual firms, or how far and how to hold directors accountable to their own employees.

There can also be conflict or apparent conflict between the values, attitudes and working rules thought appropriate in one period and another. Values, attitudes, and rules change, and in a modern economy do so with increasing speed. Experience brings new knowledge. New situations demand new rules. It is obvious that the assumptions usually made today about the

Government's duty to intervene and maintain full employment, or about the weight to be given to authoritarian as apart from participative management are very different from those of thirty or forty years ago. This is not to say that the working rules of business management are arbitrary. They rest, ideally at least, on an objective 'law of the situation' arising out of given technical, social, and market conditions. There is today a good deal of evidence that where these conditions are the same the accepted rules and conventions will tend to be similar, whether the wider culture in which particular conditions are embedded is that of, for example, the Soviet Union or the U.S.A. But as situations change and understanding of them increases, the rules objectively applicable in the light of each situation and of available knowledge about it will change as well.

To learn to cope with problems of conflict and change is another part of the training of people of sound business judgment. A director or manager needs to know when it is likely to be possible to eliminate conflict by removing a misunderstanding, how long and in what conditions wrong or simply divided views will have to be tolerated and how best to allow for them, and when it is right to fight a conflict out. If it is to be fought out he needs to know what precautions should be taken to limit the area of conflict and ensure, as far as possible, that its positive results are maximized and damaging results are prevented. He needs also to be aware of the learning process by which new ideas are mooted and worked over and finally decided upon and accepted. This process tends to proceed by a series of recognizable steps over a length of time which can often be at least roughly forecast and in major cases may extend over years. What length of time does a manager need to allow for new values and rules to emerge, be fully clarified, tested, and accepted? And what ought he to do to ensure that this process is as smooth as possible, so that new ideas are neither strangled at birth nor taken prematurely as gospel?

(e) *Permanent Values*

The ordinary working rules of business and the attitudes underlying them are what have sometimes been called 'middle principles'. They are valid for particular times and places; it may well be for long periods and in all industrial societies. Any of them, however, remains subject to challenge and change. Does this mean that permanent, universal values have no part to play in business morality? By no means: the point is more to define the level at which they play their part.

In stable traditional societies, where patterns of work and living change little from one generation to another, it is easy to make the mistake of thinking that what are in fact 'middle principles', to be dropped in favour of others when new conditions come along, have a permanent and universal value. In today's rapidly changing conditions the importance of the part played by 'middle principles' is much more easily recognized. The role of permanent universal principles, what Lady Wootton calls 'ends', is pushed farther and farther back. Ethics at one time gave the impression first and foremost of a set of permanent general rules with marginal variations around its edge. Today it presents the picture on the one hand of a mass of changing 'middle principles' and on the other of only one or two major permanent rules of a very general kind indeed, under labels such as 'respect for human personality' or the 'law of love', as the ultimate unchanging standard of reference.

But this is not to say that these alternate permanent rules are unimportant or that a proper understanding of them is irrelevant to a sound business training. In stable conditions, when the 'middle principles' applicable change little from year to year or even from generation to generation, it may not matter a great deal if people are not very clear or explicit about the final standards of judgment underlying them. They will not in any case need to refer to these ultimate standards. When, on the other hand, change becomes frequent and confusing, it becomes of the greatest importance to have explicit ultimate standards by which to steer. Kurt Lewin in one of his studies gives an outstanding illustration of the importance in unstable modern conditions of moving not only towards greater flexibility in 'middle principles' but towards a firmer and more explicit understanding of the 'ends' which provide the ultimate standard to which 'middle principles' are referred. Having left central Europe in the 1930's and moved to the United States, he was able to compare from his own practice as a psychologist the personality patterns with which typical Americans and Germans faced the slump of 1929–33, which hit both countries heavily and with about equal force. The typical German personality of those days, he suggested, was traditional, not easily adaptable at its edges and with no very firm central values. Its foundations were custom and tradition rather than strong personal belief. The typical American personality of that time on the other hand was highly adaptable at its surface levels, but this surface flexibility concealed a hard central core of deeply felt conviction. Under the strains and stresses of the thirties the American personality adapted successfully to severe and repeated shocks, thanks not only to its high elasticity in adjusting to new conditions but to the fact that its hard core of unshakeable conviction gave it a permanent, reliable point of orientation. The possessor of an American type of personality might be puzzled, but he would never be lost. The German personality on the other hand tended to crumble under heavy strain. It was neither flexible enough in its more superficial levels to discover and adapt to the 'middle principles' appropriate to new situations, nor solidly enough centred to escape being confused and misled when change and stress accelerated to the point experienced in the slump. The breakdown of German personalities was symbolized by the election of Adolf Hitler, the survival of American personalities by that of Franklin D. Roosevelt.

It is therefore very much part of training in business values to help the student to get a clear understanding of what his own central value or values are and to learn how to use this understanding as a point of reference in his more immediately practical decisions. The way in which people of different religious and philosophical backgrounds formulate their central convictions will, of course, differ considerably. A Catholic, a Protestant, a Marxist, and a Western humanist are likely to find different words to express their convictions. The content, however, is likely to be more similar than verbal differences would suggest. People of all denominations and social groups have found it possible to subscribe to a document such as the Declaration of Aims of the International Labour Office, focused on the development and welfare of human personality as the final test of action. The Declaration lays down that all human beings, irrespective of race, creed, and sex, have the right "to pursue both their material well-being and their spiritual development in conditions of freedom and dignity, of economic security and equal opportunity". When the language

of different religions and philosophies is translated it appears
that the representatives of all major currents in modern industrial societies are saying basically the same thing; that the final
test of action is its effect on the welfare and development of
human beings achieved through the development of society as
well as individuals, and of the physical and biological environment as well as of the human race itself.

WHAT IS THE BEST APPROACH TO TEACHING?

Flexible and up-to-date in his approach but knowing clearly
where he is going in the end; able to give a quick acceptable
decision with the aid of working rules and underlying attitudes
crystallized out of his experience; sensitive to the rules and
beliefs of the people with whom he deals; aware of the temporary and limited scope of his own and others' rules and of the
need to watch for and hasten change; most of us would indeed
agree that these are among the characteristics of a man whose
judgment of business values is sound. How then should the
business world and in particular those engaged in business
training go about producing such men?

A first lesson from experience is the need for an indirect
approach. American business schools have found that a sure
way to minimize the impact of a course on business ethics is to
label it by that or any similar name. 'Ethics' tends to be
associated in people's minds with the idea of old-fashioned,
rigid, and largely irrelevant rules of do-gooding and patronizing,
and of judgment rather than practical involvement. The normal
aim of management training is to encourage students to act as
responsible managers involved in a situation, who must themselves take action to bring about acceptable solutions. To
achieve this in training for production or marketing or research
is not difficult. Once, on the other hand, a course is described as
concerned with ethics or values, students tend to take the role
not of participants but of outside spectators. This feeling of
remoteness from real decisions repels not only students but,
even more, practical managers, who are also reluctant to be put
in a position where they may have to classify their own or
their colleagues' activities as 'unethical'—an unpleasant term.
Practitioners are too well aware of their own problems and of
how they themselves live in glass houses to be willing to throw

the first stone, or to incur the charge of setting themselves up as holier than their fellow-men. There is also in many managers' minds an association between traditional ethics and fixed codes of conduct, whose value today is rightly seen as small. Explicitly or instinctively, managers, like other practical men, appreciate the need today to centre ethical thinking on 'middle principles' and situations rather than on fixed and traditional rules. Like many practical men, managers themselves in any case often think more easily in terms of concrete situations than of abstractions. It is easier for them to discover principles from a case or series of cases than to learn a principle first and apply it to cases afterwards.

The basic approach to teaching about business values must, therefore, be through experience or cases and usually in a form not directly focused on value issues. In discussing, for example, the problems of advertising cigarettes the Harvard Business School's course on *Planning in the Business Environment* does not begin by raising questions such as the connection between cigarettes and lung cancer. It sets out from straightforward marketing problems in which the medical profession and the risk of cancer appear simply as two factors among many of which the advertiser has to take account. The discussion is pressed along lines of calculated ruthlessness, a process graphically described as 'testing the student's gorge level', till at last some students can stand it no longer. The discussion breaks open and the class arrives in the midst of an ethical debate on terms which give it reality and force.

It also follows that, whatever may be the case with other aspects of business training, training in business values and the way to handle them is pre-eminently a field where learning and coaching on the job count. When businessmen are asked what has done most to shape their own attitudes in this area the answer is overwhelmingly 'the example of my superiors'. There is no substitute for the personal example of a superior expressed in his own day-to-day decisions, and preferably worked out into explicit statements of the policy which he is following and to which he expects his subordinates to adhere.

How far can learning on the job be helped by guidance from outside, in the sense not so much of courses at some educational institution as of guidance directly in the performance of a manager's job? Professional groups involved in management, such as accountants or personnel managers, have or are developing their own professional standards, and bring these to bear in their own fields by education, the pressure of professional opinion, and sometimes by law. Other rules laid down by collective agreement or law also help to shape managers' understanding and application of values through shaping their practice. Company law, for example, makes clear through its rules for directors' behaviour, and for auditing, the standards of loyalty and financial integrity which managers are expected to uphold. In this and other countries there have been proposals to extend financial audits into 'social audits', reviewing a firm's responsibilities to all the parties involved in its operations and not merely (as in financial audits) to those who supply its capital, or into combined social and efficiency audits; the line between the two is not easy to draw. In those areas where managers must keep final decisions in their own hands, external rules and audits can be supplemented with voluntary consultancy.

But here there arises a practical difficulty. It is not hard to find specialists who can advise or conduct an audit on a firm's financial policy, or its personnel policy, or some other segment of its activities. What does not yet exist on any adequate scale is a body of consultants qualified to handle the whole complex of problems, including value problems, which might be thrown up by a 'social' audit, or to help with the central, overall problem of balancing together all the considerations from different fields which affect a business's policy and developing out of them a comprehensive and coherent strategy. The experience of many countries has shown that financial auditing needs to be preceded or at least accompanied by the creation of a qualified body of auditors and financial advisers. So also social auditing, and voluntary consultancy in the same area, are unlikely to be useful until enough staff qualified to undertake them are available.

At this point the needs of on-the-job training in values and how to apply them join hands with those of training in educational institutions. Staff qualified to deal both with the technical and the economic problems of business and with their value implications are needed not only for consultancy or a possible scheme of social audits, but as trainers and for business schools. At the moment very few are available, and this is the key deficiency which has to be made good if any major move towards training in business values is to proceed.

Ideally the staff needed would be qualified in terms not only of business experience, but of the relevant social sciences and of philosophy, with or without theology. The supply of social scientists able to speak with confidence on business matters is increasing steadily. A good deal of pure social-science research is in any case incidentally relevant to business problems. The work of psychologists, for example, in identifying and measuring the intensity of values and attitudes can be and is being used to give precision to the working rules of business and the values and attitudes underlying them. A few theologians have also made a serious effort to come to grips with business problems. Philosophers, on the other hand, except for a few natural-law philosophers whose approach in recent years has been un-fashionable, have not concerned themselves much with the technology of their subject and its application to particular fields such as business. There has been an iron curtain between the worlds of the practitioner and the social scientist on one side and of the philosopher on the other; and the number of people qualified to professional standards on both sides of the fence, and especially of those qualified to use techniques from both sides to analyse business problems, has been very small indeed. In American experience a particularly useful contribution to filling this gap has come from teachers qualified in fields such as arts or law who have been willing to risk their reputation by pioneering in a bridge function between two fields in neither of which they can claim to be expert. This, however, is no substitute for an adequate supply of people qualified professionally on both sides. If there is to be any major progress towards developing either teaching or consultancy in the field of business values, a top priority will be to create one or more centres at which staff with this sort of double qualification and approach can be trained to a fully professional level.

Finally, and subject to what has just been said about the essentials for training in this field—the indirect approach, the use of experience, cases, and on-the-job guidance as the main channels of teaching, and the training of properly qualified staff—there is scope for formal educational courses. But on this not much can be said in a short space, for the forms which courses relevant to training in business values can take are almost infinite. There is no one package of business-values training which can be handed out to all and sundry. What individuals and groups need will depend on the type of student envisaged—undergraduates, for example, or management trainees, or practising managers. A course may be designed chiefly to increase a student's background knowledge to give him an intellectual framework into which he can fit the knowledge he already has or will later acquire; to give him better case skills; or to equip him for teaching or research. It may focus as needed on working rules or on underlying values and attitudes. It may put the accent on the problems of the big businessman or the small, on a businessman's own decisions or on the forces in his environment to which he will have to respond. The permutations and combinations are infinite, and each firm or teaching institution must find the pattern that suits itself.

8 | Management Studies and Management Responsibilities

by RAYMOND E. THOMAS

Professor Thomas is Professor of Business Administration and Head of the School of Management at the Bath University of Technology. He was for some time Head of the Management Studies Department of the Scottish College of Commerce (now the University of Strathclyde).
He is Joint Director of the Severn Bridge Research Project and immediate past chairman of the Association of Teachers of Management.

The emergence of management studies as a rapidly developing aspect of higher and further education must pose the problems of the extent to which such studies contribute to the discussion of the responsibilities of management whether in industry, commerce, or public administration. The purpose of what follows is first an examination of present evidence as to criteria in management decisions, and second a review of the present treatment of such criteria in management courses.

To undertake this one must first establish the relationship of ideas which appear to dominate practice with the state of the theories relating to management's criteria which are currently accepted. This leads into a review of changes in management which have been in operation for a long period and which pose important questions concerning management's responsibilities. These are then contrasted with the ideas about management and its objectives that have been associated with the evolution of management research and education; in particular the partial impact of these ideas has to be recognized. Only then can we consider the role of such studies in future management education.

The Relationship of Theory and Practice

At the outset a distinction has to be drawn between 'owner-managers' and 'professional managers'. Although it is argued hereafter that the distinction is often blurred, if not totally obscured, there is merit in drawing such a distinction since it is the confusion of role and purpose of the professional manager of the modern corporate undertaking that is really so fundamental to the whole of this study. The 'owner-manager' is defined for present purposes as one whose capital stake in an enterprise gives him a dual role as risk-taker and operational decision-maker. His personal stake is of a different kind from that of the professional, largely salaried man, and this may have a very clear bearing on their respective views of their responsibilities. Thus a major aim of the owner-manager may be to preserve ownership and control in his family group, and this may influence his whole approach to expansion and change. Whether his 'proprietorial' attitudes are all that different from those of the professionals is often hard to discern. His general frame of reference is, however, that of a capitalist system, and may include a strong sense of personal responsibility for his managers and all other employees, especially where his firm is the major employer in a locality. His whole public and social life may be linked to that of his locality.

In contrast the professional manager, while having a strong commitment to his present organization, especially where features of its activities are the results of his own actions, must nevertheless have much more regard to external performance criteria, as his enterprise is subject to one of two checks. Where it is a company in the private sector the check on performance is ultimately the take-over bid which so often carries with it the implication of extensive managerial surgery, including amputation. Where the organization is in the public sector a variety of pressures are exerted by Government and public opinion and constitute such a check.

Between these pressures all managers are subject to two kinds of influence in their decision-taking, those common to all management and those peculiar to the particular society in which they have to operate. In the first category are common ideas on cost-minimization and the efficient use of resources. In the second are important influences which are often well demonstrated by the problems which confront the management of a company from one country when running a subsidiary in another—*e.g.*, U.S. firms operating in the U.K. with very different situations in industrial relations. Miss Rosemary Stewart has pointed this out in her book *The Reality of Management.*

> What managers strive for and the rules they observe in doing so will be influenced, and often determined by, the accepted goals and mores in their society. All management must be interested in profits if they are to survive in normal circumstances. But what importance they attach to them and how they seek to achieve them will vary in different societies and at different stages in the same society.[1]

Managers are, therefore, subject to the political and economic theories of their society and perhaps even more closely to those of the social groups within that society to which they tend to associate or belong. Here two comments are especially pertinent, the first being so ably presented by its author, Lord Keynes, that I feel it appropriate to quote it in full:

> . . . the ideas of economists and political philosophers, both when they are right and when they are wrong, are more powerful than is commonly understood. Indeed, the world is ruled by little else. Practical men, who believe themselves to be quite exempt from any intellectual influences, are usually the slaves of some defunct economist. Madmen in authority, who hear voices in the air, are distilling their frenzy from some academic scribbler of a few years back. I am sure that the power of vested interests is vastly exaggerated compared with the gradual encroachment of ideas.[2]

The second comment, and an equally chastening one, is that at present an assorted range of ideas is penetrating our discussions about management, stemming partly from the traditional disciplines of politics, economics, and now sociology, and partly from the study of industrial management, which was for too long cut off from the mainstream of political and economic thought during the heyday of 'scientific management'.

Any discussion must start from this point, and to explore this a little further two related movements must be considered; that towards 'professional management' and that concerned with 'management education'.

Changes in Management

In this section changes in management are considered so as to explore the challenge to both theory and practice on the 'responsibility of industry'.

The most obvious change is in the extent and basis of management, the process of 'widening' and 'deepening' of management's influence. The 'widening', the broadening of management's area of influence, is especially of concern to this discussion. The process began as far back as Robert Owen in his mills at New Lanark and has continued as successive movements, notably that usually described as 'paternalism', developed. More recently this has had two features:

> (*a*) the continuation of the provision of facilities and the anticipation of needs for which the state may subsequently accept a basic, if not a comprehensive, responsibility;
>
> (*b*) the pressure to influence first the market and then more widely in the interests of the company, as part of its survival strategy.

The related 'deepening' of management controls operates through the accelerated use of analytical techniques so as to establish data for operation and control. The extent to which this power involved a requirement for responsibility was emphasized by many of the pioneers of 'scientific management', notably Frank Gilbreth, and the subsequent problems posed by these practices have given ample proof of this need. This aspect of 'deepening' was a justification for the 'widening' in the area of social relationships and responsibilities, notably through the 'paternalism' of much 'scientific management'.

This process carries with it a whole series of assumptions as to management's rights which immediately raises questions of responsibility. The extension of skills analysis, for example, to the very elements of what the employee has to offer raises the whole question as to the employee's rights, his dependence on the manager-employer, and the extent to which he has 'property' in his skill. But here we come face to face with two sets of conditions which continue to obtain. They concern:

(*a*) the right to manage without representation;
(*b*) the 'proprietorial' role of management, even when it is salaried.

On the first of these Guy Hunter has written:

Authority, it seems, rests upon the proposition that industry, while it is a social organization, is dominated by a need for technical competence and speed of decision. Secondly, because the rights it may involve are less fundamental than ultimate political rights, the technical need may be allowed to override the current pattern of social control, namely representation. Thirdly, that authority is a part of a bargain.[3]

This emphasis on a need for technical competence and speed of decision is of course reinforced by the 'philosophy'—if that is appropriate—of 'scientific management' with its emphasis on analysis, measurement, command, and control. The one responsibility that is paramount here is that of competence.

On the second, the emergence of the company managed by persons whose financial stakes as shareholders may be insignificant and where background and experience are as salaried personnel raises the whole question of their ideology. Do these persons yet have a 'professional code' which differentiates them from the proprietor-managers either of the past or of the present day? Indeed, have such persons any consistent set of normative expectations?

The literature on this remains very thin. Successive studies in both the U.S.A. and this country have pointed to the variety of motives of such managers. Not only have they a range of material motives which are related to their assorted methods of remuneration, but they also have many non-financial motives, the search for power and influence, the sense of achievement, and the pursuit of a range of goals concurrently. Indeed, one of the characteristics of the modern business corporation is the existence of a number of objectives, each of which may be the interest of a part of the enterprise, and the reconciliation or tolerance of which is a condition of the continued existence of the total enterprise. Where they cease to be tolerated then the parts may be 'hived off' or abandoned.

Colin Marris, in his *Economic Theory of Managerial Capitalism*[4], attempts to develop an economic rationale for their behaviour. In so doing he makes three very pertinent observations. First, he reminds us of an important feature of modern large-scale business—namely, the extent to which the rewards of management are largely, if not entirely, determined by top managers themselves. This applies both to their form and level, though those of directors require formal notification by shareholders. The whole pattern of expectations and rewards is in their own hands, and they tend to continue with practices which they share partly with the proprietorial classes with which they so often identify themselves and with those in Government service. This latter observation is especially pertinent when one has regard to the bureaucratic structures of such public services and some business concerns, especially those in public ownership.

This leads to the second main comment, the extent to which such managers are concerned at the link between their own personal advancement and the expansion of the firm to which they are currently attached. This is reinforced where their attachment is such as to limit seriously their mobility in the executive market. From this it is argued that professionally managed firms have almost a built-in disposition to grow whether by direct expansion or through diversification. One responsibility is that of creating and sustaining a management team as an essential pre-condition for expansion. As Professor Penrose[5] has pointed out, the existence of a management team used to working in the particular 'culture' of the firm is essential for continued growth.

The third comment of Colin Marris on his interest here concerns the type of achievement in which managers appear to take pride. This stresses the role of change, which in turn must raise the question of how far is change preceded by due consideration of its possible social consequences both internal to the enterprise and external to business as a whole.

Yet these changes in industry, while reinforcing the power of managements—and developing countervailing powers in unions and in public policies—have left open the question of responsibilities beyond two which must now be set out:

> first, to be competent as cost minimizers/profit maximizers;
> and second, to have increasing regard for the social consequences of changes, at least as far as certain minimum

standards of treatment for existing employees are concerned.

The key questions are whether these are, in themselves, enough, given the implications of the technical, management-technical, and external-economic changes that business can see itself implementing. Part of the problem is the wide spectrum from those who are looking far ahead and facing its implications to those who still operate in small-firm proprietorial conditions.

The emergence of the modern 'business corporation' in which ultimate control is in the hands of a management group which can determine its own remuneration and succession, subject only to the threat of a take-over or amalgamation, poses several further issues: the policies of such corporations are directed towards not merely survival but continual growth through expansion of existing activities and diversification; the emphasis on internal investment is often reinforced by taxation and leads to a view of the shareholder as the ultimate recipient not of the total surplus but only of that rate of dividend as is thought appropriate by the Board in current market conditions. The choice of new investment directions is therefore more with the existing company board than with the ultimate shareholding investors.

Among the immediate implications of this are:

(i) The extent to which boards can undertake major changes, even to the sale of the company in an amalgamation, on their assessment of what is appropriate rather than on the views of the investor, and on terms which may not be the most favourable to the investor.

(ii) The role of the institutional investor and the extent to which there should be greater intervention in the management of companies by such investors, if only as a spur to greater competence.

(iii) The emergence of a common interest of the groups within the company/industry *vis-à-vis* the public at large must raise the question of the extent to which the public, whether as consumers or in any other respect (*e.g.*, prices and incomes policy), have to be considered by those making company/industry policy.

(iv) The role of the modern corporation as a patron and as a social institution contribution to 'public life'. There is a conflict of views here between those who support such activities and those who argue that directors should be debarred from employing "corporate resources in spheres for which elected representatives have assumed responsibility".[6]

Perhaps there is no better summing up of these problems than the confusion which surrounds the 'objectives, responsibilities and constraints' of a nationalized corporation which even the White Paper[7] of November 1967 does not fully clarify.

The Impact of the Study of Management

The modern manager need not confine himself, as Keynes's practical man may have done, to 'hearing voices in the air': he can go to a conference or be sent on a course. He is bombarded with exhortations and publications. In some measure these are communicating the results of observations and research, and are increasingly the subject for formal courses. What are the main ideas and what bearing have they on this discussion?

For this purpose one can identify four streams of thought which, to some extent, happen to coincide with stages both in management practice and management education in this country:

The 'Scientific Management' stream.
The 'Human Relations' stream.
The study of organization and its effect on behaviour.
The attempt to formulate a managerial theory of the firm.

The Scientific Management stream, the oldest of the sets of ideas on management, formed the basis of much of the early experiments in management education, notably in the period up to 1960, having a dominance in British management education that it had lost in the leading American business schools generations ago! It continues to be news to many smaller firms. Its implications for this discussion seem to be:

(*a*) its emphasis on management being able to obtain full knowledge;
(*b*) its implication of tighter managerial control;

   (*c*) its recognition of responsibility for social consequences
internal to the firm—*e.g.*, redundancy;

   (*d*) its assumption of a 'common purpose';

   (*e*) its disregard for much political and economic theory.

A development from the reaction to the above, the Human
Relations stream, emphasizes the individual, the need to recognize his needs, the existence of informal organization and controls, and it makes a major inroad on managerial omnipotence
by conceding the need for more participative management.
This stream still has strong influences on management/supervisory training from TWI onwards, and is responsible for a reinforcement of the recognition of a responsibility to 'look after'
employees. Yet the continuation of industrial conflict and the
speed of changes in organizations make this insufficient. In
particular there is often an inconsistency between this approach
in training and the real situation of the trainee.

The impact of the social sciences on studies of organization
and behaviour is an extension of the Human Relations school.
Studies in this group have focused attention on the problems
of interacting social systems and organizations in business and
other situations, on the need to understand the values and
objectives of those involved, and on the conditions necessary to
create a climate of opinion which will be more capable of digesting, if not of stimulating, change. Such approaches contain even
bigger challenges to the earlier views which can be seen in
several ways.

Perhaps the most fundamental change is the move towards
alternative management styles in which the emphasis is on a
more participative or consultative pattern. The aim here is to
secure greater involvement of people not only by enabling them
to contribute ideas and indirectly formulate at least interpretations of policy, but also to share in setting the measures of their
own performance through such target-setting practices as
'management by objective' and such considerations of managerial styles as are implicit in the 'management grid' approach.
The extent of involvement must raise questions of values and
objectives. Indeed, certain studies of participative management
experiments have shown these to test the ability of such systems
to cope with decisions which are repugnant to the participants.[8]

With this goes a much greater emphasis on the forward planning of the enterprise, especially in terms of its capital and its
manpower needs. The latter carries an implication as to the use
of the social scientist in anticipating the social consequences of
technical and managerial changes.

The emergence of management education has passed through
the phases of controls and control techniques, social skills and
organizational studies to come to the core of the subject,
managerial ideology, objectives, responsibilities, and constraints.
At the same time the largely descriptive study of the social and
economic framework within which business operates, supported
by a reappraisal of theories of the firm as studied in economics,
leads towards some managerial theory of the firm. This last
point is well expressed by Shirley Cleland:

> The traditional theory of the firm considered the firm as a
> passive reactor to market events, intent upon maximizing
> profits. The managerial theory of the firm considers the firm
> as an organized information system intent upon a satisfactory
> profit but operating in an external and internal environment
> which allows the manager significant decision-taking power.
> . . . The aim is to have time to plan for the future growth,
> power and insight to attempt to influence his external
> environment . . ."[9]

The Role of Management Education

The issue to which one is now brought is therefore what
should be undertaken in the emerging provision of management education to at least provide a forum for discussion on
this theme. To approach this, two sets of comments, one relating
to American management or business education and one to
British practice, are necessary.

A feature of the American business schools is not only the
emphasis they give to the study of Business Policy through case
studies, executive seminars and simulations, but the attempt to
provide a background of teaching on what is best described as
the "way of life of American business". There is an attempt to
spell out in some detail not only the competitive ideal but the
social responsibilities of business. Texts and course materials
include analyses of such issues as 'local community relations',
'international relations', and 'employee responsibilities'.

Such activities are consistent with many features of American society and American higher education. The far higher standing of business as an activity and of management as a career in American society is reflected in the scale and level of education for business. While it is true that such American undergraduate business studies attract poorer students to essentially vocational careers, the postgraduate schools of business and industrial management set a very high standard of attainment. The curricula, while covering in depth the 'technology of management', also emphasize the question of objectives and responsibilities, though the latter are often a continuation of the promotion of the 'American way of life' as part of the process of nation-building.

In Great Britain the emphasis, with some university exceptions, is on 'the technology of management', ranging from work study to econometrics, and on introducing the student to the methods of studying organizations as political and social institutions rather than as presenting a formal course in business ideology or responsibilities. The problem here is the confusion and uncertainty of those who have to operate in what is traditionally a very pragmatic society, having a wide spectrum of ideas.

The purpose of this essay is to present these problems rather than to provide a guide to action, whether in management education or elsewhere. Discussion and research can undoubtedly help us better to understand the complexities of industrial management, but I remain sceptical of our ability to emerge with any very clear outcome. If we can only appreciate the forces at work and the essentially political problems to which they lead, then this will be a worthwhile achievement. Management has its own mythology. Study can at least remove the more dangerous myths.

[1] R. Stewart, *The Reality of Management* (Heinemann, 1963), p. 129.

[2] J. M. Keynes, *The General Theory of Employment, Interest and Money* (Macmillan, 1936), p. 383.

[3] G. Hunter, *Studies in Management* (University of London Press, 1961), p. 102.

[4] C. Marris, *Economic Theory of Managerial Capitalism* (Macmillan, 1964).

[5] Edith Penrose, *The Theory of the Growth of the Firm* (Basil Blackwell, 1959), Chapter 9.

6 Alex Rubner, *The Ensnared Shareholder* (Macmillan, 1965; Penguin Books, 1966).

7 White Paper on Financial Performance of Nationalised Industries, November 1967.

8 For example, the critical issue of redundancy in the Standard Motor Co. at Coventry cited by Seymour Melman in *Dynamic Factors in Industrial Productivity* (Basil Blackwell, 1956).

9 Boulding and Spivey, *Linear Programming and the Theory of the Firm* (Macmillan, 1960), Chapter 7.

9 | Values and the Employee

by FERDYNAND ZWEIG

Ferdynand Zweig was born at Cracow, in Poland. He studied Law and Economics at the Universities of Cracow and Vienna and at the London School of Economics. He graduated as Doctor of Law at the University of Cracow. Dr Zweig became Professor of Political Economy at the University of Cracow before the War and economic adviser to the late General Sikorski, war-time Prime Minister of Poland.
Since the end of the War he has devoted himself to the study of the British working classes, publishing a series of studies such as *Labour, Life and Poverty, Men in the Pits, Productivity and Trade Unions, Women's Life and Labour, The British Worker, The Worker in an Affluent Society*.

Value orientations are the determinants of human motivation, consequently also determinants of attitudes and behaviour. Their study is far from easy, as they form a conglomeration of conscious and unconscious elements at various depths. They also form a combination of cognitive elements consisting of images of reality and affective-directive elements, expressed in norms as guides to action with various degrees of sanction. Both cognitive and affective-directive elements are closely linked with each other, as the norms are based on the images of reality, on the way we see it and interpret it to ourselves; and the moment the images change, the norms also change direction.

Values are deeply rooted in the past, but with social change they also undergo a process of transformation. In fact, with the quickening pace of social change we are witnessing today a process of deep metamorphosis of values.

Value orientations are also a *sui generis* combination of collective elements, what is called 'shared values' (*i.e.*, values shared by members of a collectivity at various levels) and individual elements (*i.e.*, personal values based on individual experiences), each sphere considerably influencing the other.

The system of values of the employee on the shop floor—namely, the worker—with whom we are concerned in this paper, is, of course, a conglomeration of both collective and personal values, of both past and present, of both conscious and unconscious forces, of both cognitive and affective-directive elements. The forces and elements in question may be convergent, reinforcing each other, but they are more often in conflict, pulling in opposite directions and causing anxiety and insecurity in the mind of the worker. In present-day society the worker is more than ever torn between those forces, especially between the past and present, between conscious and unconscious elements, between collective values as represented by his class consciousness and personal values as represented by his self-interest and self-determination. The (almost) affluent society is different from the scarcity economy governed by grinding poverty, the democratic society differs from the society based on class privilege, the fully employed[1] Welfare State from the individualistic State based on mass unemployment. The class consciousness was based primarily on common struggle, deprivation, underprivilege, and sense of injustice; the new pattern of society which is emerging strengthens the forces of individuality, which have gained considerably in post-War development. Those forces made vast inroads into the traditional mentality of the worker, enlarging the field of permissiveness and liberalizing the sanctions of the norms evolved in the long period of collective struggle. But with all that the worker still remains basically a loyal member of his class with a fair measure of what we call class consciousness, and identifies himself with his class. The British worker is still basically a 'collectivity oriented' individual (to use Talcott Parsons' term), whose system of values is primarily based on the collective experiences of his class—*i.e.*, the class of people who earn their livelihood by working with their hands.

Images of Reality

Before we can analyse the core of the system of values as embodied in the norms we have first of all to inquire into the images of reality relevant to the worker's situation. We have here a whole progression of images of various degrees of generality.

First of all we have a general image of social reality as a whole, as the worker sees it around him. Does he see his society as predominantly based on solidarity and mutual help, justice and equity, or does he see it as a battlefield of greed, selfishness, and violence? Of course, it is a question of emphasis rather than a clear-cut choice.

This image will basically colour all other images of lesser generality. If a man sees the world around him as a play of greed, selfishness and violence, he will behave very differently from a man who sees the world as an ordered universe basically governed by fair play and equity.

The working-class image of the social universe has been basically pessimistic, but it has undoubtedly improved in the Welfare State with full employment and relative affluence.

The subsequent images which will influence the worker's attitude and behaviour may be divided into two separate sections: section A concerning the world of business and section B concerning his own social class and his workmates.

In section A the first image concerns industry at large. Does the worker see industry as a Leviathan, grim, blind, and uncharitable, aiming at producing maximum profits out of the sweat of its employees, or does he see industry as a co-operative national venture which has a most significant contribution to make to national progress, security of the country and its position in the world, providing work and welfare for all? Of course, it is again a question of emphasis rather than a clear-cut choice. Here the governing idea which will influence the worker's behaviour is his belief in the existence or absence of exploitation as the general principle of industrial action.

The collective image of industry among the working classes has been traditionally sombre and highly overcast with fears, suspicions, and resentment, but no-one can deny that it has enormously improved in post-War development. The problem of nationalized industry has shown the nature of profits in a different light. The public concern, and also the concern of the Labour Party and Labour Government, with industrial growth as the basis for expansion of social services, for defence, for foreign policy, as well as employment, has greatly affected the traditional image of the capitalist as a wolf or shark. The worker begins to see the other side of industry as the key to national progress and development.

Next in progression comes the image he beholds of the company in which he works. It is based partly on his own personal experiences and observations and partly on those of his workmates and the reputation of the company in the labour market. It is again viewed in terms of emphasis in the pairing of opposites. Is the company out for maximum profits at the expense of its employees, or does it consider the security and welfare of its employees, deviating from the law of profits by paying due regard to social and communal interests? Is management in all its grades fair and just, giving equal chances to everyone, or is it inclined to favouritism? Is the company organized effectively as an efficient, highly productive working force, to which it is worth while to make a positive contribution, or is it badly organized, ineffective, and inefficient? The image of the company will be summarized in one sentence: This is a good company to work for, or vice versa. This image will have a vital influence on the worker's attitude and behaviour on the shop floor.

Of course, this image varies considerably from firm to firm, according to working conditions, organization, and quality of management, but by and large we can say that in most progressive companies the image which the worker beholds of his firm is at present more favourable to his firm than before the War. It is partly due to the spread of collective bargaining, improvement in working conditions, fringe benefits, personnel service, and human-relation techniques.

Lastly in this section we come to the image which the worker beholds of his own job, viewing it against his chances and possibilities. Does the job, if he is a skilled man, offer him full opportunies to use his skill and for advancement; if he is not a skilled man, is the job a man's job, which gives him self-respect and status? How does the job compare with other jobs within his range in terms of pay, hours, health, security, fringe benefits, his family commitments, etc.? This image will be summed up in a sentence: a job worth keeping or a job of little value. This will have the most powerful effect on his attitudes and behaviour on the shop floor.

The post-War development has influenced this image in many divergent ways. Full employment and some welfare services have extended the choice of jobs available to average workers and made many inferior jobs in industry not worth keeping.

On the other hand, for higher grades of labour and for those employed in more progressive companies offering differentially better terms, full employment has strengthened the bond between men and the company, making those jobs a very worth-while asset.

Now comes section B. In this section the first and most general image concerns the working class as a whole. Does the worker see his class as a mass of under-educated and ill-equipped men concerned only with their narrow interests and benefits, as selfish as everybody else, or does he see his class as in the *avant garde* of progress, social justice, and equity, with which he identifies himself completely? In each case his attitude and behaviour towards his workmates and superiors will be different.

The traditional self-image of the working class is in post-War development a little blurred, and the image has lost some of the pristine beauty of St George fighting with the dragon, but still most workers see the working class as the class which gives to the community more than it takes from it, a class which stands for justice, progress, and social betterment. Even if the worker sees the world as governed by greed and selfishness, in most cases he would exclude his own class from this image, regarding it rather as the object and victim of greed and selfishness than as the participant in the scramble for gain.

Next in progression comes the image of the trade unions and especially of the trade union to which he belongs. For long periods the union has been treated as a sort of *sanctum* in the worker's life, and it is still basically a cherished and well-appreciated institution. But the unions have grown into giant administrative national bodies with huge bureaucracies which are often far removed from the rank and file. As national bodies they assume national responsibilities, and have often to protect national interests against sectional interests of their members. Instead of institutions of struggle and conflict they become part of the Establishment. They often assumed the role of 'leaders of men' instead of advocates of their interests. They often have to side with employers and the Government[2] against the demands and claims of their members. This was the case even before the wage freeze, which gave an additional shock to the image of the unions.

Full employment is another factor which makes the union less attractive to its members, as the unions are often acting as

H

a restrictive factor in the 'wage drift'. But although the image of the trade union is blurred and a little tarnished, it still remains basically the workers' institution, without which the worker cannot help to achieve his full status in industry, to which he aspires.

Finally comes the image the worker beholds of his mates in the company in which he works, and more specifically in his own team, in the so-called 'small' group. His mates can give him a sense of belonging and fellowship, they can give him support, both in emotional and social terms, they can make his work pleasant and satisfying, or they can be obnoxious, suspicious, and vindictive, and make his work troublesome and burdensome. The actual image which the worker beholds of his workmates will determine his measure of identification with his working group, which has a strategic central position in his behaviour on the shop floor. The 'small' informal group can act as a corrective to the formal groupings controlled either by the management or by the trade union; it can work in harmony with them or it can set itself against them.

Of course, the image can vary with each company, team, and individual according to their experiences, but the collective experience of the worker *per se* has built up the image of the workmates in warm and most appealing colours, as the most valuable asset of the working man. In post-War development this image has undergone certain modifications coming from very divergent and conflicting forces. One force which blurred the warm and positive image of his workmates is the growing individualization of the worker. He sees himself more as an individual, pursuing his own self-development, his rights and interests, more specifically his pecuniary interests. Full employment, the car, television, often his house property, the rise of educational standards, all those factors have to a large extent taken him out of the mass and made him also emotionally and mentally more independent. Conflicting with this is the need to band together in pursuing sectional and trade interests, which previously were defended by the trade unions. As these joined the Establishment, often pursuing national interests, they left a vacuum which is being filled by informal groupings at the shop-floor level. Also the development of fringe benefits and the practice of work consultation increased the need for banding together of small groups directly involved in a work situation.

The balance of these forces is very difficult to assess, but on the whole the collective image of his mates which the worker beholds is still painted in warm and attractive colours.

The Norms

Those were the cognitive elements of workers' values, sketched in very broad lines. Now we come to the affective-directive elements, to the analysis of the norms (or 'desirables' or 'oughts') accepted as valid by most workers on the shop floor. They are based on the workers' interpretation of reality, and they follow closely the findings about the images described in the two sections: one section of images painted in cool, withdrawn colours, the other section of images in warm and attractive colours. The main source of the norms in question is the working-class mystique combined with the ethos of the trade union and the *esprit de corps* of the 'small' group. Also in the field of norms we can see a certain progression from more general norms with a wider range of validity, which we will call principles, to more detailed and specialized cases, which we will call rules.

The first two basic principles, which are complementary to each other and strongly supporting each other, are the principle of conflict in the worker-employer relationship and the principle of workers' solidarity in this conflict.

The principle of conflict proclaims that the worker-employer relationship, although both are involved in a joint productive venture, is basically governed by conflict. This conflict arises out of the fact that both the work process and the distribution of the product of work are controlled by the management. And so the conflict arises out of the division between those who give orders and those who receive them and out of the division of the fruits of labour between profits and wages. The management represents a force of considerable magnitude which has to be counterbalanced by a countervailing force of workers' organization based on solidarity. The countervailing force has to keep in check the authoritarian control of management of both processes, the work process and the distributive process. The second principle, the principle of workers' solidarity, declares the identity of the interests of the workers *vis-à-vis* the employer and their obligation to support each other's claims through a united front.

From those two principles follow a number of rules of conduct, some institutionalized in customs and union rules, others in formal guide-lines, which have to be observed under the penalty of being classed as a 'blackleg' or 'scab' and in more severe cases being 'sent to Coventry'. Not all the rules apply with equal strength to all grades of labour, to all industries and all situations, and not all of them have an equal sanction. Some have a larger latitude of permissiveness than others, and all find themselves in the process of liberalization. Most rules are in the nature of injunctions or restrictions, but some are in the nature of claims against the employer or resistance against his action. In broad outlines they can be described as follows:

(1) The rule of non-competition with workmates—for instance by exceeding the group output norms or by offering excess overtime work or by courting favours with the management in any possible way.

(2) The rule of not showing up the weaker or less efficient or less skilled man.

(3) The rule of non-complaining about workmates' behaviour or against informing management about blameworthy actions of workmates, except under duress.

(4) The rule of not putting other men out of a job—for instance, by taking on an excessive workload or manning more machines.

(5) The rule against swamping the labour market by the employment of unskilled workers instead of skilled, juveniles or women instead of men, or exceeding the accepted ratios of apprentices to skilled trades.

(6) The rule of promotion by seniority or seniority with ability, opposing the practice of promotion at the sole discretion of management, which often degenerates into favouritism.

(7) The rule of dismissal in case of redundancy by an agreed rota—e.g., last in, first out—not by arbitrary choice of management, again meant as a bulwark against favouritism.

(8) The rule against paternalism. What is given as favour or charity and not of right is rejected.

(9) The rule against non-organized workers. The rule calls

for refusing to work with non-union workers, as far as possible, as those weaken the bond of solidarity and gain benefit from organization to which they do not contribute.

(10) The rule of 'brotherly' code of conduct *vis-à-vis* workmates and members of the union, calling for friendly, helpful, and co-operative patterns of behaviour.

(11) The rule of discipline calls for disciplined behaviour, especially in cases of organized conflict, supporting those who are in the forefront of the conflict.

Another important principle, which reinforces the previous two principles mentioned, is the principle of fairness. It stems not only from working-class consciousness, but also from the world of the Bible consciously or unconsciously absorbed, and last but not least from the world of sport, which has an enormous impact on the workers' mentality. The words 'fair' and 'unfair' are always on the workers' lips. The ideas of fairness are mostly based on long-established customs and habits, if they are favourable to the workers, or on standards accepted in the trade generally. Any deviation from the standards of pay, hours, or conditions generally accepted in the trade is regarded as unfair.

From the principle of fairness follow many rules, such as:

(1) The rule of equal chances. The management must give equal chances and equal opportunities to all men on the same job or in the same grade. The rule applied to workmates calls for giving any member of the team a chance to prove himself.

(2) 'A fair day's work for a fair day's wage'. It implies fairness to the employer in giving him the stint customary in the trade. It implies fairness to the craft by giving full consideration to the accepted standards of quality in the trade. But it implies also that if the worker is not paid what he regards as a fair wage he is not obliged to give a full equivalent.

(3) The rule of customary wage differentials between various grades of labour, which should be maintained

as far as feasible. This applies especially to the differentials between skilled, semi-skilled, and non-skilled labour. The worker is not an egalitarian in the sense of the Aristotelian principle of 'arithmetical justice' (everyone the same), but rather subscribes to his principle of 'geometrical justice' (according to grade and merit), as more recently elaborated by George C. Homan in his theory of distributive justice (proportionality of reward to 'costs' and 'investments' of the worker).

(4) The rule of the customary workload. The customary workload should not be exceeded without the consent of the workers and proper compensation.

Another important principle is the principle of dignity. This principle asks for treating men not as 'manpower' or 'living tools' but as human beings with the respect and dignity due to every human being in a democratic society. This principle has been enormously enforced in post-war development with the rise of general standards of education and the deepening of democratic awareness. It is expressed, for instance, in the practice of renaming menial jobs of a humbler class, such as lavatory attendants or garbage-disposal men or cleaners. Many firms have made the discovery that if they give a more dignified name to a menial job of this kind they can achieve better results in recruitment. The name of a job is especially important for signing agreements for hire purchase or in mortgage contracts or for introducing oneself on outings or on holidays.

The whole field of supervision, previously governed by the 'tough line' school of thought, has been affected by the quest for dignity. Giving orders by shouting, "Do this, do that", has been replaced by more dignified forms implying co-operation and guidance. The principle of dignity turns against all authoritarian styles of supervision and management, encouraging more democratic forms and styles.

The same principle demands also consultation—both formal and informal—with men on the job, previous to any substantial change affecting their job. It demands equally providing the men with all the information concerning their job's prospects in the future. A foreman who complains, "I am not informed", says in fact, "I am treated as nobody"; keeping 'in the know' is part of the quest for dignity.

Complying with the principle of dignity is not only conducive to good labour relations but also to a firm's progress and productivity. The greatest danger to industry is apathy, passivity, and self-estrangement of the worker and his belief in the meaninglessness of the industrial process—what is called the alienation of the worker, not his will for participation, which is the outcome of the principle of dignity.

The principle of security of job was not very strongly stressed among workers' values in previous periods, when mass unemployment and poverty were rampant, but, curiously enough, it has considerably gained in force in the affluent society. A worker no longer leads a hand-to-mouth existence. Most workers have been fully employed since the end of the war and have adapted themselves both psychologically and economically to this condition. The fully employed Welfare State encourages what is called 'consumer orientation'. The young worker tries to reach early the 'standard package' of a fully-equipped home, often with a car and his own house, by easily entered commitments on hire purchase. All this makes the worker very sensitive to all fluctuations of his income and very security-conscious. Accordingly, demands for longer-term notices of dismissal in case of redundancy, for redundancy indemnities and compensation, and for longer contracts of labour are made more and more.

Finally we come to the principle of improvement, which became an important value in post-war development. This principle states that living standards ought to improve from year to year. This is implied in what is often called 'the revolution of rising expectations'. The worker's appetite for good things is whetted; he wants more. When asked about his possessions he often uses the term "Next on my list is . . .". The traditional standard of living is outmoded.

Accordingly the rise of wage rates should not only make good the rise in the cost of living, but should also include a 'co-efficient of improvement'. Growth of national economy and growth of the respective companies are implied in this requirement. The economy ought to be dynamic enough to absorb the constant rise of wage rates, and companies which are unable to comply with this requirement must fall in the struggle for survival in this new age. This is a new and very important element in transforming the traditional pattern of the economic system, which is confronted with a new challenge.

Conclusions

I have described here the value orientations of the worker in very simplified and broad lines in a model or 'the ideal type' form, but they are of a much greater complexity in various degrees of combinations of both images and norms. Not all the values have the same validity for all groups and types of workers, for the young and for the older men, for the higher and lower grades, and for all sections of industry. Not all value systems professed by the workers have the same consistency and integration, as presented in the model form. Man's mind is a battlefield of ideas, of images and norms which sway him hither and thither according to collective and individual experiences. Man as a partial universe often finds himself in a dialogue between various centres of his personality representing divergent value systems 'interiorized' in his own consciousness and coming from various sources absorbed often unconsciously.

The most important dialogue takes place between the self and the collective consciousness interiorized into oneself. The dialogue often assumes the form of a dilemma, or an outright conflict with feelings of anxiety, *malaise*, and uncertainty, about which path to follow. The results of the dialogue are expressed in a compromise or straight victory of one side or the other. The relative strength of personal *vis-à-vis* collective values depends on numerous factors, both subjective and objective. Among the subjective factors the most important is the strength of the worker's personality, his self-confidence and self-esteem. Only a strong man can boldly proclaim with a touch of arrogance and aggressiveness, "I am what I am and I think what I think". Among the objective factors the most important is the divergence or convergence between personal and collective experience, as expressed in his specific situation in the firm and on the job. Some men find the old collective experience reproduced in their own personal experience, others not. In a good, well-managed firm and well-appreciated job his own personal values may approximate on many points to the values of management, which are also 'interiorized' by the worker to a degree. The degree depends on the image he beholds of the firm and his job. We see how complex are the value orientations of the workers. They form a real orchestration of operative values in action, with many instruments to play in various situations and times.

For the time being the social change seems to strengthen values based on personal experience of the worker, on his image of the company and his own job, at the expense of collective values, but this does not necessarily mean that this process will continue also in the future. Much depends on the direction of social change in time to come. Here the operative forces are first of all full employment, economic growth, and further development of the tools of industrial democracy in action.

The social reality is after all the matrix of consciousness, and any change of reality is reflected sooner or later in both images of reality and ensuing norms. Here the emphasis is on 'sooner or later'; the time lag between change in reality and change in consciousness is of the very first importance. Their congruence in the long run ("in which we are all dead"—Keynes) is not a safeguard against maladjustment, rigidities, and waste. Hence there is ample scope for industrial education to help in bridging the time lag.

The study of values is only in its infancy, and although up to now it has only scratched the outer layers it has already uncovered large vistas and perspectives in the understanding of human motivation. As a method of study it possesses a great potential. "The matter of values", as Clyde Kluckhohn intimated, "is certainly the prime intellectual issue of the present day".[3]

REFERENCES

George C. Homan, *Social Behaviour* (London, Routledge, 1961).

Josephine Klein, *Samples from English Cultures* (London, Routledge and Kegan Paul, 1965).

Clyde Kluckhohn, *"The Study of Values"*, in a symposium *Values in America* (University of Notre Dame Press, 1961).

Clyde Kluckhohn, *Culture and Behavior* (New York, The Free Press of Glencoe, 1962).

Talcott Parsons, *The Social System* (New York, The Free Press of Glencoe, 1951).

F. J. Roethlisberger and William J. Dickson, *Management and the Worker* (Cambridge, Mass., Harvard University Press, 1943).

A. Zaleznik, C. R. Christensen, and F. J. Roethlisberger, *The Motivation, Productivity and Satisfaction of Workers* (Harvard University Press, 1958).

—— *Human Dilemma of Leadership* (New York, Harper and Brothers, 1966).

F. Zweig, *The British Worker* (London, Penguin Books, 1952).

—— *Productivity and Trade Unions* (Oxford, Blackwell, 1951).

—— *The Worker in an Affluent Society* (Heinemann, 1961).

[1] The unemployment rate in August 1967 was 2·4 per cent of the labour force, the highest since 1940, but still below what the Beveridge Report regarded as full employment.

[2] To mention only the TUC–CBI initiative of productivity and its relationship to the National Economic Development Council and the 'Little Neddies', the Industrial Training Board, and to the Minister of Labour's National Joint Advisory Council, etc.

[3] *Culture and Behavior*. (The Free Press of Glencoe, 1962), p. 287.

10 | *The Ethics of Persuasion*

by RAYMOND J. LAWRENCE

Professor Lawrence graduated from Cambridge with a degree in Classics and Economics. He entered Unilever as a management trainee in 1950 and stayed twelve years on the marketing side of the business in Britain, France, and Australia. Before leaving for a period of study in America he was for three years Advertising Manager of J. Kitchen and Sons Pty, Ltd, a Unilever subsidiary company in Australia responsible for soap and detergents marketing. He worked for two and a half years in the Ph.D. programme of the Graduate School of Business Administration, University of California, Berkeley, taking marketing and consumer behaviour as his special subjects. After returning to England in 1965 he was appointed to the first Chair of Marketing set up at a British university—at Lancaster.

Persuasion is the task of the two major business functions, selling and advertising. Both activities are designed to cause desired action, usually buying action, to be taken by others. Expenditure on persuasion is very substantial. In Great Britain £600 million was spent on advertising in 1966 and probably as much again or more on field sales forces, an input total equivalent to 3–4 per cent of the country's gross national product.

Strangely enough, it is not the *economics* of persuasion which attract most attention, even among businessmen. Accurate costing, work study, journey cycle and callage frequency analysis, sales potential estimation, demand forecasting, and other techniques are not often applied to the field sales force. Advertisers mainly work by rule of thumb and hunch, setting their budgets as a fixed percentage of turnover and relying on 'experience', which, as Oscar Wilde said, is the name everyone gives to their mistakes. The voices of directors crying to high heaven "Are we getting value for all this money we are spending?" are lost in the babble of debate about the *moral* aspects of persuasion. Advertising is the favourite subject. Public controversy and potential Government legislation revolve around the issue of whether advertising is wasteful, dishonest, and lacking in taste. We are a moralizing country, happier with inconclusive argument in the old debating tradition than with hard, numerate evaluation.[1] The consequence is that managers are more likely to be questioned on the ethics of their activities than on their efficient use of resources.

Why should persuasion generate such heat? To anticipate the argument developed later, it is because the objectives, methods, and effects of persuasion cut across a strongly held value system at almost every point. The value system can be called the scientific-rational. In attitude-theory terms it is powerful because it is a higher order system or referent which colours a host of interconnected sub-attitudes toward such things as sensational Press headlines and political speeches, religious ritual, and holiday camps. Rationalism has not been studied by psychologists as a personality syndrome with the thoroughness devoted to ethnocentrism or the authoritarian personality, although economists are familiar with the idea of Rational Man. Unfortunately this mythical creation has, like Franken-stein's monster, shown an unexpected capacity for independent existence and activity. He is part of a false, over-simplified dichotomy of human mental processes which is still influential. His worst crime may have been to discourage investigation of a genuine phenomenon. Because Rational Man readily collapses on critical examination, behavioural scientists are disinclined to search the debris for usable material and prefer to look else-where. If the view taken here is correct, persuasion and persuas-ive techniques are offensive because they violate an Image of Man which is closely tied to scientific, rational values. The values themselves have, of course, a long history, running back to the Milesian philosophers and the great forebears of modern scientific rationalism—Bacon, Descartes, Spinoza, and Leibniz. It is the effect of holding the common modern version of belief in rational principles which has not been adequately studied.

Persuasion may enter into any form of information-conveying communication, to join Desmond Morris in using the term to exclude what he calls mood talking, exploratory talking, and grooming talking. The first serves to convey the emotional state one is in. Instead of yelping or roaring a human being can say, "I am hurt" or "I am angry". Exploratory talking is an aesthetic or play activity, using words as a poet does for the joy of verbalization. The third category deals with such phenomena as cocktail-party conversations. When two primates meet and one wishes to signal that this is to be a friendly, sociable encounter he grooms the other by cleaning his fur. Morris suggests that the meaningless, polite chatter of social occasions serves the same purpose. It is not concerned with exchanging information, revealing mood, or giving aesthetic pleasure. It is simply a way of passing the time while signalling friendly intentions, the equivalent of primate grooming.

Within the field of information talking the first ethical issue which arises is that of motive. The persuader is partly suspect because he has some personal axe to grind. But this is not the whole story. The bishop or missionary is not regarded in the same light as the door-to-door salesman, although both may be equally absorbed in persuading others. The difference seems to lie in the nature of the interests served: whether they are 'higher' and non-personal, or selfish. The moral issue is the status of self-interest.

If persuasion is used for self-interest and self-interest is wrong, then persuasion would stand condemned. The great religions have tended to regard the body, the personal self and the present as barriers impeding the way toward the life of the spirit, the divine mystery, and the hereafter. As the American economist George Stigler caustically puts it, "a dislike of profit-seeking is one of the few specific attitudes shared by the major religions". The Christian ideal of the humble servant working only for others has been particularly hard to make stick, as the historical record shows. Probably most people today would admit self-interest as legitimate providing that it does not go over into gross selfishness and disregard for others. The fact is that *everybody* tries to influence other people in his own interests, except perhaps the true saint and other isolates. The baby at the breast soon learns signals to induce his mother to behave as he wishes. Young children are adept at behaviour designed to influence others—for example, to gain their attention. It is not usually accepted that these actions are immoral. In normal maturation the process of ego formation consists of exploration, observation, and manipulation—and it is timely to draw the fangs of this sinister word: finding means to get others to act on one's own behalf is normal and natural, a part of the child's development and exploration of his own powers. The word 'manipulation' is used because it has emotional overtones, suggesting some sort of unhealthy objectives or methods. It will be necessary later to examine whether there is a valid basis for the implication.

Religious people may take self-interest as part of original sin, to be gradually overcome by personal effort. But, in addition to religious values, social and scientific values are hostile to the cult of individual interests. Part of the split between industry and the universities is on the ideological issue of objectives. Industry accepts money-making and profitability as desirable goals. The academic world is inclined to scorn mercenary purposes and to claim the pursuit of knowledge for its own sake as an objective. The individual scholar is not seeking prestige or reputation (and least of all an increase in salary), but subordinates himself to the pursuit of truth and the development of his subject. By this standard, self-interest and personal aggrandizement tend to be regarded as undesirable motives, and the idea of communication as a vehicle for one man to do himself some good at the expense of another appears particularly obnoxious.

Every person has to take his own view of the legitimate boundaries of self-interest. Adam Smith, who was a moral philosopher before becoming a political economist, regarded it as the only reliable motive in mankind. If the would-be persuader is to be condemned for looking after himself, in fairness the same condemnation should be applied to all instances where self-interest motivates behaviour. The range of such activities will be found to be very wide.

There are more specific points, however, which highlight persuasive tactics as reprehensible. Some of them are related to the methods of persuasion. Information talking may be split up into elements called arguments. An argument can be defined as a perceptual unit, equivalent to the cognition in attitude theory. "Queen Elizabeth I ascended the throne in 1558", "Beer is best", are arguments. They stand somewhere between the micro units of phonemes and words, the building bricks of linguistics and grammar (which in turn can be analysed in the bit units of information theory), and the aggregate units of attitudes or bodies of knowledge about a subject. Any communication is a set of arguments. Thus the message "A tiger is coming. Climb a tree quickly", is defined as a two-argument communication. One of the complaints about persuasion is that the set of arguments selected is *biased*, in two main ways. First, *suppressio veri*—some of the arguments which 'should' be included are left out. Secondly, *ad hominem*—in the special sense that the set of arguments is selected to work on a particular target audience. Persuasion could in fact be defined as the communications process by which one party adduces a subset of arguments, out of a set of all arguments related to a subject, selected to have an effect on another party in a desired direction.

Now the selection process, if it is regarded as undesirable, must clearly be contrasted with a fair process which is the proper way to present a set of arguments. Difficulties arise in trying to define such a process. It cannot consist of putting forward the complete set of arguments, because they are too numerous. The dilemma is familiar to the historian. Any significant past event is so surrounded with commentaries, and commentaries on commentaries, that an exhaustive listing would be impossible or unreadable. Even *Which?* comments on products can only cover some of their characteristics. A subset of arguments has to be chosen, and choosing implies principles of choice, which in turn imply objectives.

In this light the famous distinction between information and persuasion can be examined. Alfred Marshall was responsible for emphasizing the difference between constructive or informative and combative advertising, and his analysis still seems to be attractive in many quarters. The key issue is whether there is such a thing as 'pure information' which exists, as it were, objective-free. Apparently simple statements of fact usually imply a purpose. "The 10.05 train from Euston reaches Glasgow at 16.45 hours" is one of countless arguments about this daily event. A poet or a schoolboy would find many alternative aspects of the train to comment on. The timetable-compiler selects the argument most relevant to people wishing to travel from London to Scotland. With a million arguments to choose from he selects this one. His choice is determined by a communication objective. How pure is the information? It is clearly intended to affect other parties in a desired direction. Timetables are not published for fun or in a spirit of indiscriminate philanthropy. There is an element of self-interest in the example, however. The statement "Water boils at 100°C" sounds more unexceptionable, for the physicist who makes it obtains no personal benefit, but he is also applying criteria. He is presenting us with one argument out of countless others. Water also has characteristic behaviour at 90°C or 61.472°C. We are not told about this because basically a value judgment has been made that the temperature of transition from liquid to gaseous state is important or useful information. An effect is desired, the passing on to others of worth-while data. The closest approach to pure information is that of the scientist who devotes himself to evaluating, say, silica compounds, although there are no known applications. He can then offer his results to the world without thinking of their current usefulness. But he must also have the purpose of adding something valuable to human knowledge, for, if he did not, there would be no point in committing his results to paper. More knowledge would be gained, though not transmitted, if he continued with his experiments instead.

Once it is admitted that human objectives enter almost inevitably into the communication of information, the notion of pure or dispassionate factual information becomes weaker. Objectives can change over time as new fashions and philosophies arise, and within one individual a mixture of personal objectives normally interact with each other. Objectives imply 'a desired direction' in which the reader is to be led, and arguments are selected accordingly. The writing process has in it an element of persuasiveness or subjective purpose, a distinction depending on definition, but the two terms are not far apart.

Difficulties in separating information from persuasion have been looked at from the writer's point of view because this is less familiar ground. At the reader end of the communication link the task is easier. The psychology of duality between a rational and an emotional part of the human being is no longer popular. The mind operates as a single unified system, and it is impossible to categorize arguments as appealing only to one or the other of two distinct types of mental process.

Subjectivity instead of objectivity and self-interest instead of unselfishness come together in persuasive communication, which suffers a double condemnation by ethical judgments derived from religious or scientific-rational value systems. By other lights persuasion is not necessarily seen as a Bad Thing. The ancient Greeks, for example, valued the effective orator. Nestor and Odysseus won their reputations partly as able speakers. The sophists, those much-maligned teachers, offered lessons in forensic skills. Aristotle taught rhetoric and wrote several books on the subject. But a great gap seems to have followed the classical period. The art of persuading people has not been systematically investigated until modern times with the work of Hovland and his colleagues at Yale, although their work is concerned with the effects of communication on attitude change rather than with the techniques of persuasion. Certain individuals, of course, have been brilliant persuaders. British political and religious leaders furnish many examples, but these seem to be cases of personal flair. They do not constitute attempts at close analysis of the principles of persuasive communication.

Taking up an earlier point, persuasion is disliked because of bias in the presentation of arguments. Only the factors favourable to one side and unfavourable to the other are produced. However, the objection often fails to take into account the *structure* of the total situation within which the persuasive arguments are advanced. By convention it can be agreed that opposing interests are represented by strictly one-sided arguments, while the adjudication function rests in other hands. This is called the advocacy system. It is familiar in the courts of law, where counsel for the defence and prosecution put forward the case for their respective sides in order to persuade a judge or jury; and in the procedure of debating societies and political parties, where partisanship is an understood convention and the object is to influence votes.

Unfortunately a certain disreputableness seems to attach to advocacy methods. For one thing, the professional advocate is distrusted because he is prepared to take either side of a case. In fifth-century Athens one of the serious charges against Socrates was that he taught ways of making the weaker cause appear to be the better one, and he paid with his life for the unpopularity of the sophists who did exactly that. Like a modern lawyer, they would take a brief from either party and, for a consideration, make out a strictly partisan case. Probably the jury which tried Socrates would share two vaguely formulated ideas with the man in the street today: first, that there is something wrong when the presentation of a case affects its outcome—especially when the presentation involves slick arguments that are deliberately put in to sound good although they are incorrect. Second, that there must be a 'right' side to every dispute, so that the man who is prepared to put his services at the disposal of either side must be a scoundrel. The first of these attitudes represents partly the average citizen's distrust of people with faster brains than he has. The second attitude is made up of two fallacies: that there is some absolute 'right' answer, instead of shades of grey on both sides, and that the advocate 'ought' to be a truth-seeker impartially weighing up the evidence.

Dr Johnson can help us get our thinking straight on the ethics of advocacy. Boswell asked him whether there was not something dishonest about the legal profession because a lawyer might have to support a cause which he knew to be bad. The Doctor answered:

> Sir, you do not know it to be good or bad till the Judge determines it. I have said that you are to state facts fairly; so that your thinking, or what you call knowing, a cause to be bad, must be from reasoning, must be from supposing your arguments to be weak and inconclusive. But, Sir, that is not enough. An argument which does not convince yourself, may convince the Judge to whom you urge it: and if it does convince him, why, then, Sir, you are wrong, and he is right. It is his business to judge; and you are not to be confident in your own opinion that a cause is bad but to say all you can for your client, and then hear the Judge's opinion.

This is an admirable answer. Johnson distinguishes the two functions of judge and advocate, and points out that it is quite inappropriate for the advocate to act as his own court of law and, for example, to refuse a brief because he may not feel that right is on his client's side. There is always something to be said in a man's favour, and the lawyer's responsibility is simply to find it and say it.

The same argument can be used to defend advertising and salesmanship against one of the criticisms made against them. The promoter is in the advocate position where his role is to find out the favourable things to say about his product and to say them. He is not also to be the judge in the situation. That is the customer's job. The situation is well structured, and the conventions are widely understood. A seller is known to be urging a partisan case, and the prospective buyer can make allowances accordingly.[2] An objection can legitimately be raised if the structure of the situation is *not* made clear. This is the case of the advertisement which is deliberately designed to be taken as part of the editorial matter of a newspaper, of the salesman who pretends to be an adviser or market research investigator, of subliminal advertising. The reason for stopping such practices is that they misrepresent the situation to the customer and lead him to expect a different set of conventions to apply.

While on the subject of misrepresentation it is time to stand up and be counted on the issue of falsehood in persuasion. The case for accepting the conventions of the advocacy system has been urged, implying the acceptability of a deliberately selected set of arguments. It is not suggested that the same licence be extended to untruthful or misleading arguments. A mechanism is needed to prevent the use of false claims, for, even if 'the truth will out' in the long run, in the short run too much damage can be done by misrepresentation. The mechanism needs to be effective, implying some form of compulsion on offenders as a last resort, and it needs to be in continuous operation to judge the grey-area cases and establish interpretations of principles on a case-law basis. Whether the mechanism is established by the State and legislation or by voluntary self-regulation within the industry opens up a wide subject which cannot be fully discussed, but two general points can be made. First, precise legislation is exceedingly difficult. The British Code of Advertising Practice begins "The Code is to be applied in the spirit as well as in the letter", recognizing that detailed rules tend to create a cycle of evasion and new legislation, with the evaders normally one jump ahead of the legislators. Broad statements of principle, like those of the Sherman Act, are perhaps all that can be attempted, even though the crucial task of application then devolves on the adjudicators. Second, the scope of control should be limited to falsehood, deception, and misleading statements. The ethics involved are close to those of the ninth commandment, not some general paternalism aimed at protecting a defenceless public from the wickedness of advertisers.

The second objectionable element about persuasion is that arguments are chosen to 'match' the requirements of a given situation. Aristotle defined the art of rhetoric as the ability to discover the means of persuasion *in each particular case* and, like Plato in the *Phaedrus*, discussed audience psychology. Such tactics are reprehensible to the rational-scientific school of thought, which tends to believe that all truly rational men will reach the same conclusion given the same evidence, and that there is broadly only one correct way of presenting the evidence—*i.e.*, with a maximum of scientific objectivity. On this view persuasion can add nothing to a judgment process except the false notes of emotionality and special pleading.

The rationalist philosophy can be treated as either descriptive or prescriptive, as dealing with what is or with what ought to be. As description the philosophy has been heavily undermined by the work of psychologists from Charcot, Le Bon, and Freud onward. They see reason serving more powerful and primitive forces as a lackey, supplying rationalizations and 'good reasons' for behaviour while the actual source of motivation, the 'real reason', lies elsewhere. Nothing is more dismal than to see executives trying to apply arguments which are logical from their own standpoint to situations where powerful emotions and feelings are involved on the other side. Redundancy and restrictive practices are cases in point. Much of our educational system is devoted to indoctrination into rationalistic thinking: it is not surprising that engineers often fail to cope with human and group problems where slide-rule logic is inadequate as a basis for understanding what is going on.

The prescriptive viewpoint that men ought to be rational is an ethical issue. The major religions do not enthrone reason among the cardinal virtues. Philosophers from the time of Pythagoras have been the protagonists of rationality, which is deeply enmeshed in the scientific value system. If men ought to be rational, it can be argued that they ought not to be susceptible to persuasive arguments. A distinction needs to be made, however. An argument may be persuasive if it is a *new* one to a particular individual. Some fact of which he was previously unaware can change his view. The imprecise border between information and persuasion again comes to light because the persuasive power of an item of information is clearly a function of the elements already in an individual's information set. Persuasive power does not contradict rationality if it derives from new evidence. But even if the rationalist admits that persuasion may legitimately operate in this way, he is likely still to harbour hostile feelings arising from three sources: ego defensiveness, the Honest Worth attitude, and anti-emotional bias.

The first might be called the 'implied criticism' complex. If someone is trying to change my views and there is a chance that he is right, then the opinion which I currently hold is less than adequate, and I am therefore not as clever as I thought I was. This is apt to be an uncomfortable sensation. The persuader often gives his victim the feeling of being 'got at', of being shifted from his cosy preconceptions. In extreme cases a strong ego defensive reaction can be provoked, leading to anger, withdrawal, derogation of the source of the new material, or other means of dealing with dissonance, to use Festinger's term. The good salesman is aware of the dangers of putting his case too strongly, especially in dealing with insecure individuals who readily interpret powerful arguments as a form of personal attack. More generally, listening to new or contrary points of view implies some risk of having to adapt existing attitudes or else to man the defences with scepticism, laughter, disbelief, etc. Attitudes are by definition a relatively stable organization of cognitive and affective elements, so that the persuader can easily be seen as a threat to the established equilibrium.

The Honest Worth attitude has a moral element, since it expresses a feeling about the way the world should be organized. Many people believe that solid merit, honesty, craftmanship, and personal integrity should win recognition unaided. Virtue does not need the meretricious assistance of Public Relations. In a manufacturing context the world will beat a path to the better mousetrap-maker's door, as Emerson is credited with observing. Undoubtedly the Honest Worth standpoint is praiseworthy in many cases. The artist may stand by his personal vision and hope to obtain recognition after his death. The process of time winnows away the temporary successes of the day and brings to light the work of enduring value. One of William McPhee's most intriguing models indicates that music is rich as an art form because the retention rate of the best music is very high, whereas television lapses into banality because its retention rate of the best material is relatively low. When Kai Lung mentioned the divine assurance that integrity would in the end prevail, the woodcutter Shen Hing replied, "In the end? . . . Admittedly. But an ordinary person inclines to something less ambitious provided it can be relied upon more towards the middle.'' In other words, the decision to await the long-run outcome is a question of personal courage, but it is unrealistic to expect that short-run or medium-run benefits will accrue as well by some sort of automatic justice. Recognition depends on factors outside the area of an individual's moral decision such as fashion trends, good reviews, and sheer luck. The Honest Worth attitude, in fact, implies quite considerable smugness about where the responsibility for recognition lies. It is up to the outside world to make all the running, to be seeking merit, to honour it where it is found and to make its fame known. The Honest Worther does not stretch out a hand to assist the communication process. He is entitled to do so if he genuinely rejects the opinion of the outside world as worthless. The ethics of the rights of the individual to choose his own way of life raises fundamental problems, but some of the practical consequences are well known. The artist is liable to a life of poverty. The businessman devoting himself to the perfection of hand-made brassbound widgets can find himself in bankruptcy. The outside world responds to neglect with neglect. Honest Worth which does value external opinion must, these days, also play an active part in the two-way communication process with its public. The artist may need the help of a gallery to provide him with an exhibition. Universities and research institutes can demonstrate the value of their activities instead of assuming that their virtues will shine with pure, internal light. Businessmen need marketing skills mainly to drive home the lesson of communication, both *from* the customer to learn about his requirements and *to* the customer to make known how his needs can be met. It has been justly remarked that the world is not beating paths to doors any more.

A third objection to persuasion arises from the anti-emotional bias of scientific-rational thinking. The idea that the passions and senses are dangerous, misleading, and false goes back to the pernicious Plato. Probably today the condemnation of emotional appeals still rests fundamentally on a distaste for the emotions as such. An advertisement telling a woman "You will get a little lovelier each day if you use product X" may attract intellectual scorn as being unconvincing, improbable, or downright false. But the objection may go beyond logical and aesthetic criticism to an ethical judgment, that the desire to be beautiful should not be part of female motivation. Similarly the desire for prestige, the satisfaction of ownership, and other sentiments can be regarded as morally undesirable. The handling of emotions is, however, at least as much a social as a moral issue. Children are taught to restrain their temper, greed, and selfishness in order to make a reasonable social life possible. Among adults conventions prescribe the expression of emotion: Anglo-Saxon men may not weep in joy or sorrow, but Latins allow themselves to do so. The adjustment between individual rights to emotional expression and the rights of others is an empirical one, achieved by a social consensus. It seems better to treat the handling of emotions by social rather than by moral criteria. The issue is a very real one. For example, the British Advertising code states that advertisements should not play on fear or superstition. But what about greed, or envy, or feelings of inferiority? Appeals linked to these emotional reactions may be effective persuaders. The portrayal of violence on television is a closely related issue in that 'undesirable' excitement and interest in fighting may be provoked. There is a shortage of research into the question whether emotional arousal in one context makes it (*a*) more likely to occur in another context or (*b*) less likely to occur, through an Aristotelian catharsis or purging away of the emotions in question. Some work has been done by observation of violence in children's play following exposure to filmed material, but it does not answer the general question. Lacking information, we must make our decisions on ethical or social consensus grounds. In the former case some emotions will be categorized as wrong or bad, not to be portrayed or aroused. It seems preferable, however, to rely on the mechanism of convention. Advertisers and salesmen are obliged to work within the limits of the commonly acceptable since otherwise they will not achieve their objectives. The occasional exception serves to show how very much of an exception it is. For example, a newspaper on one occasion published an advertisement which suggested that sympathy be extended to some types of drug-taking. The editor did not refuse to let the item appear on the moral grounds that it was wrong. However, perhaps he might eventually do so, given evidence that repeated insertion of the material was offensive to a large body of readers. In the case of a relatively new subject the line is hard to draw. With more familiar issues the general location of the line is better known, and the mass media can steer clear of material which would be generally felt to be indecent, blasphemous, obscene, degrading, or otherwise unacceptable.

The subject of emotion leads on to another important problem. Some people feel that advertising and salesmanship are objectionable because they put desires into people's heads which would not arise otherwise. Vance Packard has a chapter called "Progress through Planned Obsolescence", and discusses the enticement of the consumer to buy artificially differentiated, 'unnecessary' products. The underlying idea seems to be that there is some list of possessions which it is right and proper to desire, corresponding to another list of 'basic human needs'. Psychologists have had singularly little success in defining the latter. Hierarchies of wants or needs are given by such writers as Allen, Maslow, and Murray, and there are many more. Unfortunately all the lists differ, and all are equally useless for the translation of needs into precise means of satisfying those needs, for there is no one-to-one correspondence between them. 'Need for food', 'hunger drive', 'survival motives' appear on most lists, but the labels do not tell us what people will actually decide to eat. At first sight it seems attractive to specify a dietary minimum as the basic need, calculated by food specialists from measures of work to be done. But this line of thought breaks down in other less quantifiable areas. Clothes may seem necessary in cold climates, but nudists will point out that they are not 'really' necessary, given an adequate diet. By a sort of compound aestheticism the truly primitive requirements come down to something like a daily handful of rice, a figleaf, and some friends. Diogenes had all that a man needs.

The fact is that the social environment mainly determines human wants and goals. Today we regard a certain level of sanitation and hygiene as basic. Our ancestors were quite unaware that such needs existed. Discussing the distinction between luxury and necessary goods, Christina Fulop asks, "In which category, for example, would one place central heating, instant coffee, frozen foods and detergents, to mention only four post-war products?" The 'needs' terminology is indeed nonsense, but there remains a feeling that it is improper to want too much. Americans in particular are accused of striving excessively for material possessions. If there is something wrong in always wanting more, then advertisers might be blamed for dangling ever more attractive carrots before the deluded donkey.

A very important point of social philosophy is at issue here. Should satisfaction with the *status quo* be the objective at both the individual and community level? If so, powerful educational and social forces can be brought to bear with the object of making each citizen content with what he has. Thomas More's *Utopia* postulated such a society, which comes closest to realization in highly formalized types of social organization where the appropriate level of material possessions is specified for each individual. Scorn, ridicule, and disapproval are used to bring the ostentatious and ambitious into line. The case is well known of native South Americans and Africans who will work for wages for three months, then return to their villages for the rest of the year because they have met their needs of a bicycle or a bride price. This outlook is not regarded with favour by Western employers, and yet it is perfectly logical. Given limited wants, the worker is satisfied when he has met them. Presumably he is happier than his employer who would like a better job, more money, and a new car. A value judgment between the two philosophies has to take into account the correlates of each, however. The tribal society is apt to be static and inflexible. Innovation and new methods of production or disease control are not likely to be easily introduced. The Westerner will probably set out to get his new car by working harder, reducing costs, finding profit opportunities, and bringing in new ideas. It seems reasonable to assume that the correlates are an inescapable part of the package. The philosophy of contentment and satisfaction could in theory go with social dynamism and adaptability, but in practice it does not do so. In some sense a choice has to be made of the type of society one prefers. If McClelland is right such a choice is sometimes made simultaneously by many achievement-motivated individuals who carry their community forward to new heights of prosperity. Spain in the fifteenth century, England in the sixteenth and nineteenth centuries, the U.S.A. in the twentieth, are examples of societies which have found for a time new power to explore, invent, and develop resources. Discontent rather than satisfaction with the *status quo* is part of the driving force. Ernest Dichter makes discontent a major theme in the introduction to his book *The Strategy of Desire*: "If we assume that it is part of the basic nature of life, man, and man's place in this world to change continuously and constructively, then creative discontent is a healthy goal of persuasion and education." It does appear that more wants rather than fewer are needed for the achievement of material progress. New and modernized consumer goods are the inducements offered by a free-enterprise economy, and may be the major factors in socialist and communist countries. Intellectuals may prefer other and nobler social goals than economic welfare, but material possessions and freedom of choice appear to be important to the general public in the long run, as opposed to moments of ideological excitement.

The argument to this point has assumed that the presentation of inducements is a relatively neutral process. The wage-earner sees publicity for colour television sets and decides whether to work and save to buy one. If he does so decide it is because he has made a free choice among many alternatives and found this one to be the best. The situation would be very different if advertising had the power to *force* an individual to buy television. Dichter distinguishes command and persuasion as methods of causing action to occur. But perhaps the two overlap: excessively powerful persuasion, as in the case of Chinese communist brainwashing techniques, might make nonsense of the free-choice postulate and amount to a means of control.

Views about advertising effectiveness are remarkably polarized. On the one hand, publicity is seen as an all-powerful agent, capable of dragooning a helpless public into buying whatever the large corporations choose to sell. On the other hand, advertising is despised as ineffective frivolity and a waste of money. There are those who manage to adopt both views at once, believing that advertising is a powerful influence on other people but entirely without effect on themselves. A paper by Weinberger throws some light on the latter point: it appears that people who say they are little influenced by advertising in fact respond almost as positively to the suggestions of television commercials as the public at large.

'High-pressure salesmanship' is also believed to be a powerful force. The phrase itself is an interesting indicator of stereotyping, along with expressions like 'stuffy offices', for the vast majority of salesmen do not use pressure tactics, for the simple reason that they generally do not work. None the less, the Hire-Purchase Act, 1964, gives the consumer three days within which he may legally withdraw from a contract signed in his home (as distinct from a shop), presumably so that he may have time to recover from the impact of a sales pitch and have second thoughts. The theme of Eugene Burdick's novel *The Ninth Wave* is excessively skilful manipulation in the field of politics. The central character, Mike, knows how to exploit secret weaknesses and fears in individuals and, through market research, among groups of voters. The other main character is so overwhelmed by the power Mike possesses that he finally kills him.

It is clear that there is considerable public uneasiness about the power of persuasion. The issue bears on ethics because it sets the scale of the problem. If persuasion is enormously effective the moral questions involved are more acute. For example, if advertising for cigarettes causes thousands of people to start smoking who would otherwise not have done so, the rightness of permitting such publicity is a more urgent matter than if advertising only affects brand preference and not the decision to smoke.

The evaluation of advertising effectiveness is a subject of great complexity, but at least there is enough evidence to negate the hypothesis that propaganda is all-powerful and allows its users to control their markets. Empirically, large and supposedly sophisticated companies have made disastrous blunders in launching new products. The Ford Edsel is the classic case. Unilever's Lyril toilet soap, Strand cigarettes, General Mills' cereals, many Birds Eye frozen food lines, are other examples. Perhaps large firms would like to be able to execute Galbraithian or Packardian manipulation, but they lack the skill and power to do so. Psychological theory indicates that the consumer is well equipped with selective perceptual defences, and attitudes on important issues are difficult to budge. Joseph Klapper, after an exhaustive review of the evidence on communications effects, came to the conclusion that the mass media had little influence except to speed up changes which were occurring anyway, owing to other factors. Habit, tradition, and inertia are strong brakes on rapid change.

Even taking the extreme example of deliberate efforts to change a person's beliefs and values—the techniques known as brainwashing—a cool look at the evidence by Dr Lifton, Kinkead, and others has shown that there is no new dimension of thought control available to political authority. Given complete power over a prisoner for weeks and months, our ancestors were equally good at extracting confessions from all but the most obdurate.

The lurking worry about being tampered with or manipulated, so successfully used by Vance Packard and others, is perhaps connected with fears for the ego and the resistance to suggestion so evident in the three-year-old, who asserts himself against authority and resents having the way prepared for him by others. Such worries will lead to the feeling that persuaders *may* one day develop powerful and subtle methods, even if they have had not much success so far. The argument cannot be denied any more than it can be proven. However, the criticism based on some potential threat can be met with Aristotle's defence of rhetoric: "If it is argued that someone who knows how to use the power of words might do great harm if he used his power unfairly, the same argument applies to the misuse of any good thing." Scientific knowledge, political strength, and industrial capacity are all powerful forces which have the capacity of being used for good or evil. Only a few people would argue for their elimination because of the possibility of abuse.

Even if persuasion has relatively little effect in major matters except to lead the public in a direction in which it was moving anyway, it can be argued that whatever small power persuasion has is to the bad rather than to the good, and that suppression would therefore be desirable. Even if only a dozen people are persuaded to smoke by advertising, their harm is reason enough. When the importance of the ethical issues is scaled down, however, other social values enter the picture. Economists from Marshall and Pigou to Kaldor, Telser, Scitovsky, Firestone, and others have attempted to weigh up the advantages and disadvantages of advertising. They have tended to be unfavourable, particularly when their thinking has been loaded with the notions of pure competition, perfect markets, and rational choice. Typical demerits are the raising of distribution costs, the creation of barriers to new entry, the distortion of consumer preferences, and wastefulness. On the other side the advantages of mass production, standard quality and reliability, speed of innovation, and the support of media vehicles are stressed. It is unnecessary to produce one more attempt to establish the balance of economic advantage. But, taking a wider view, limitation of advertising, promotional and selling activities implies a social philosophy which has effects extending well beyond the immediate aims of such restrictions. The status of the market economy and scope for individual enterprise, relative freedom of action for firms and individuals, business confidence generally, enter into the picture. Karl Popper defines the main task of the theoretical social sciences as being "to trace the unintended social repercussions of intentional human actions". It is precisely the unintended repercussions of restricting promotions and competitive action which need the most careful consideration.

Finally, persuasion is frequently condemned for its use of methods. False enthusiasm, exaggerated claims, trickery in presenting the case are quoted even if the accusation of downright falsehood is withheld. On the first point Dr Johnson can again throw some light. In the passage quoted Boswell went on to ask:

"But, Sir, does not affecting a warmth when you have no warmth, and appearing to be clearly of one opinion when you are in reality of another opinion, does not such dissimulation impair one's honesty? Is there not some danger that a lawyer may put on the same mask in common life, in the intercourse with his friends?"
JOHNSON: "Why no, Sir. Everybody knows you are paid for affecting warmth for your client; and it is, therefore, properly no dissimulation: the moment you come from the bar you resume your normal behaviour."

Salesmen and advertising-agency personnel are aware of the implied Contamination Theory which underlies many reactions when, in a party conversation, they reveal their line of business. But, like the lawyer, they can be honest men. False enthusiasm and exaggeration clearly do not pay off if they are perceived as such. What usually happens is that each individual has his own views about what is convincing and believable. He cannot easily credit that other people have different standards. As for trickery, it will always be true that some individuals are persuaded by unsound arguments. No legislation can altogether prevent fools and their money being quickly parted. A better counter-weapon is exposure of the tricks. It might be argued that the tricks can be stronger than the truth: the deceptive appeals portrayed in cigarette-advertising are more powerful than the facts about the bad effects of smoking, for example. Aristotle had the answer when he wrote that, given that truth and justice have an innate superiority over their opposites, then if they fail to influence decisions it must be because they are badly presented. In other words, the man with truth on his side has a permanent advantage. If he loses out *it is his own fault*: he has failed to use the techniques of persuasion as well as his opponent. This is surely the correct view, although its implications may seem distasteful. Government departments, research institutes, nationalized industries, and other august bodies would have to learn how to match the persuasive methods of their opponents, to descend into the arena, to send men on such unheard-of courses as training in creative copy-writing. In fact, it might be no bad thing, judging from the notably unpersuasive effects of so many official instructions, advisory booklets, and reports recommending action by others.

In practice the arts of the persuader are likely to continue in disrepute because they clash with scientific-rational values. The main differences between the two systems can be summarized:

	Persuaders	*Scientific Rationalists*
1. Motives	Self-interest, gain.	Pursuit of truth.
2. Effects sought	To induce action desired by the communicator. 'To win'.	To state a case fairly. 'To play the game'.
3. Roles	Advocate, partisan.	Judge, critic.
4. Materials used	Biased subset of arguments.	Representative or fair subset of arguments.
5. Audience influence	*Ad hoc*. Arguments tailored to audience.	Uniformity, prescribed by rational or scholarly tradition.

6. Tone of presentation	Reinforcement by emotional appeals sought.	Reinforcement by emotional appeals avoided.
7. Merits	Realism, effectiveness.	Idealism, honesty.
8. Weaknesses	Unscrupulousness.	Inappropriateness to situation requirements.

If they can never achieve respectability, however, the persuaders have a number of compensations. For they are the empiricists, the practical operators in the world that is, rather than the self-deluders in the world of ought-to-be. When the rationalizing committees have finished deploring the foolishness of the public at large in failing to drive carefully, to pick up litter, to join the Army, or whatever it may be, they may have the sense to abandon their dignified appeals and call in the persuaders. If they know their job properly, these men will set about establishing what people really know and feel about the issue in question. They will work inductively from facts, not deductively from preconceptions. Aneurin Bevan once said that the use of market research would take all the romance out of politics. Perhaps the romance has departed, for the parties now rely on finding out which issues really concern the public. Normally they turn out to be domestic and local ones, not international politics and ideological debate. Finding out the actual state of public attitudes is a starting-point, a better one than guesswork and casual chat within a restricted circle, but it is only the beginning. The creative work of finding the words and pictures which will cause the desired action to take place then has to be done. It is in this area that the professional persuaders are apt to go adrift. They have little real understanding of habit formation, learning processes, channels of influence, reference standards, and many other aspects of human behaviour. Emphasis is placed instead on the creative idea *per se*. Some gifted people such as David Ogilvy can produce advertising which is both original and effective, but in most campaigns the dimension most easily identified is the one which runs from play-it-safe mediocrity to harebrained originality-at-all-costs. Among representatives, too, there are many mere order-takers and casual, ill-informed salesmen. In fact, one could wish that the persuaders would espouse their own ethic more strongly and get better at their business. There is perhaps too much of apologetics and hat-doffing towards the rationalist value system, which occupies a proud and noble place but cannot claim to offer the only 'right' criteria for worth-while endeavour. Britain's economic position at least would benefit from more good persuasive methods and fewer neatly balanced Civil Service arguments.

In the contrast between reason and persuasion many threads can be seen which run through long periods of history. There is the contrast between the idealist and the realist, the prescriptive and the descriptive. On another level similar elements distinguish the thinker and dreamer from the practical operator, the other-worldly from the worldly. The position of the sophists, those much-maligned teachers, may offer the closest parallel to the persuaders. They also suffered from a two-pronged attack. From one side the intellectuals represented by Plato disliked them for teaching useful career skills for money; on the other side the mass of the people distrusted them as being too clever by half. Yet they acted as a valuable leaven, promoting change and new ideas (Bertrand Russell points out that the translation which best represents their occupation at the time is the word 'professor'). The modern pejorative sense of sophist and sophistry derives from the bad associations of money-making, cunning argumentation, and a practical, applied approach as opposed to an interest in ideas for their own sake. In our own times the same associations attach to the arts of persuasion. It seems that intellectuals and the public join in a distrust of this combination, if for different reasons. After more than two thousand years perhaps it is time for our attitudes towards persuasion to develop in a less antagonistic direction, for the possibility of persuasion is part of the price we pay for a relatively free society and democratic institutions.

REFERENCES

William A. Belson, *The Impact of Television* (London, Crosby Lockwood and Sons, Ltd, 1967), p. 365.

Desmond Morris, *The Naked Ape* (London, Jonathan Cape, 1967), pp. 202–206.

George J. Stigler, *The Intellectual and the Marketplace* (Chicago, University of Chicago Graduate School of Business Selected Papers No. 3, 1962), p. 7.

Adam Smith, *Wealth of Nations.*

Boswell, *Life of Johnson*, Vol. iii, Chapter 2.

Alfred Marshall, *Industry and Trade* (London, Macmillan, 1919), pp. 304–307.

J. A. C. Brown, *Techniques of Persuasion* (London, Penguin Books, 1963), pp. 20–21.

Leon Festinger, *A Theory of Cognitive Dissonance* (Row, Peterson and Co, 1957; Stanford University Press and Tavistock Publications, 1962).

William N. McPhee, *Formal Theories of Mass Behavior* (New York, The Free Press of Glencoe, 1963), pp. 26–73.

Ernest Bramah, *Kai Lung Unrolls his Mat* (London, Penguin Books edition, 1937), p. 13.

Leonard Berkowitz and Edna Rawlings, "Effects of Film Violence on Inhibitions against Subsequent Aggression" (*J. Abn. & Soc. Psych.*, May 1963), pp. 405–412.

Vance Packard, *The Wastemakers* (London, Longmans Green, 1961).

C. N. Allen, "A Psychology of Motivation for Advertisers" (*J. Applied Psych.*, XXV, 4, August 1941, pp. 378–390).

A. H. Maslow, *Motivation and Personality* (New York, Harper, 1954).

H. A. Murray and others, *Explorations in Personality* (New York, Oxford University Press, 1938).

Christina Fulop, *Consumers in the Market* (Institute of Economic Affairs Research Monograph No. 13, 1967, p. 61).

David C. McClelland, *The Achieving Society* (Princeton, New Jersey, D. Van Nostrand Co., Inc., 1961).

Ernest Dichter, *The Strategy of Desire* (London, T. V. Boardman and Co., Ltd, 1960), p. 13.

Martin Weinberger, "Do People Know how Susceptible they are to Television Advertising?" (*Public Opinion Quarterly*, summer 1962, pp. 262–265).

Eugene Burdick, *The Ninth Wave* (London, V. Gollancz, Ltd, 1956).

Joseph T. Klapper, *The Effects of Mass Communication* (New York, The Free Press of Glencoe, 1960).

Eugene Kinkead, *Why they Collaborated* (London, Longmans, 1960).

Robert J. Lifton, *Thought Reform and the Psychology of Totalism* (Norton, 1961).

Aristotle, *Art of Rhetoric*, 1355b and 1355a.

Karl R. Popper, *Conjectures and Refutations* (London, Routledge and Kegan Paul, 1963), p. 342.

Bertrand Russell, *History of Western Philosophy* (London, George Allen and Unwin, Ltd, 1946), p. 94.

[1] William Belson writes of "a predisposition, perhaps a peculiarly English one, to settle matters of social significance on the basis of argument and armchair wisdom".

[2] The reader may care to make up his mind between the view expressed here and the opposite case put by J. A. C. Brown: "There is nearly always something concealed by the propagandist. What he conceals may be his real aim in engaging in his campaign, the means (suggestion and other psychological techniques) employed, the fact that there are alternative views to his own, or the fact that if these are mentioned at all it is only to misrepresent them." Brown apparently recognizes only scientific objectivity as a 'proper' method of conveying information.

11 | *Theology and Work*

by G. R. DUNSTAN

Professor Dunstan is F. D. Maurice Professor of Moral and Social Theology at King's College, London; a Canon Theologian of Leicester Cathedral; Editor of the monthly Journal *Theology*.

The request for a Christian ethics of a particular activity—like work—is often a mistaken request. At least, the request may have to be formulated anew in different terms before it can properly be answered. For the Christian claim is not to a peculiar way of life for a peculiar set of people whose ethical questions are answered for them in advance in their sacred books. The Christian claim is to the means of insight into what is true for all men. The means are grounded in an awareness of the God who chooses to reveal to men first himself, as one with whom men may have fellowship, and so also that purpose for men which his own nature requires. In knowing him, furthermore, men gain knowledge of themselves and of their solidarity as men.

Thus a Christian answer about work may not be given, without preliminary, in terms of "This is what a Christian ought to do". It must be given first in terms of what is, in some sense, 'natural' to man: proper to his nature and to the conditions of his life on earth. Granted the wish for survival, both corporate and individual, work is a compelling necessity for mankind. Platitude as this may be, the words are necessary to anchor the discussion in the elementary facts of life. Individuals and isolated minority groups may manage to live without working themselves; but they do not live without *work*, other people's work, which alone produces or has produced the wealth on which they subsist. Whether the work was that of slaves or of a subjugated people or class, or whether it is that of a modern industrial labour force making and setting in motion more and more sophisticated machines, wealth remains a product of work, however much the condition and quality of the work may change.

Work is thus an economic society. From our position in an industrialized, and now increasingly cybernated, society in the second half of the twentieth century we can look back across millennia in which work has meant unremitting toil. The old Biblical phrase, "subdue the earth", throws up an accurate picture of struggle, toil, conquest, exploitation. A living has been wrung from and from beneath the soil; from the forests hunted, cut back, burned; from the swamps drained, the seas sailed and fished; from rivers harnessed; from wind, from rain, from fire. For a majority of mankind today life still demands this struggle with a soil which, overcrowded and over-exploited as now it is, yields rapidly diminishing returns: the race between the retreat to sterility and the bringing of the technical aids to soil fertility and economic revival is now on; the pace is swift, the issue uncertain—fatally uncertain, for in the race itself millions die undernourished and many starve. In Western Europe and its off-shore islands the home-born, the settled, buy their freedom from the public drudgeries of life increasingly by means of the employment of migrant and immigrant labour; unintentionally, perhaps, but effectively, we tend to keep some immigrant groups, not indeed in servitude, but in socially depressed conditions of life which hinder their proper absorption into society. These are warnings enough from the U.S.A. of the disasters which can flow from this. When, for instance, technological development, and particularly cybernation, reduces the demand for human labour in some processes, it is the socially underprivileged and those with least education and technical skills who are the first to become unemployed, and then, if left to themselves, unemployable; for cybernation requires that those fewer workers who are employed be skilled.[1] To be workless, to be a member of an involuntarily workless group, is to be in a condition of social deprivation with consequences far more disastrous than those of being overworked. Whether considered in terms of economic survival or of personal integrity, the necessity of work is part of the condition of man.

A 'theology of work', therefore, does not begin with a statement that men ought to work; but with a recognition that they do, and that they must. The theological concern is what we make of, and with what we do about, this universal fact. Is work a curse or a blessing? Or is it both curse and blessing? If a curse, is it redeemable, is it redeemed? If a blessing, is it corruptible, is it corrupt? If it is both, what imperatives are we to utter, what persuasions are we to institute, in order that its blessing may be rich and its curse without power? These are the first questions which theology asks about work. About its product, wealth, and about the distribution of wealth, further questions would be asked in turn; but they lie beyond the range of this essay and must be left for another.

Curse or blessing? The question is posed at the very beginning of the literature of the Judaeo-Christian tradition, in the earliest chapters of Genesis: though this is not to say that these were the earliest written. The first two chapters of Genesis record, in the magnificent language of myth, or symbol, or parable, the grappling of religious minds with this fundamental ambiguity of human life. (And how magnificent is that language—how far removed from the triviality with which it is sometimes read, discussed, and dismissed—is fittingly expressed in the music to which Haydn set it in *The Creation*.) The whole creation—firmament, earth, seas, forest, field, bird, beast, man—is the work of God, marked at every stage with his word of pleasure, of contemplative satisfaction, in what has come into being at his command. God is the worker, breathing pure delight in the recognition that his work is good. And man is made a worker too: he is set in the midst of this firmament, and given dominion over it; he is set in the garden of the world, to till it and keep it. And tillage is work. The whole creation is blessed with fruitfulness; but the fruit will not be harvested without work. Work is part of the blessing; man is blessed for work, and work blessed for man. This is the first, symbolic, parabolic, word of the Bible: one side of the ambiguity. On the other side stands the curse, expressed also in symbol in the next chapter of Genesis, the third. Man and his wife together disobeyed a clear command—clearer to them, perhaps, than to us; and so they lost dominion, lessened their beatitude. This parable speaks not of tillage but of toil; not of blessing but of curse; not of the herb and the tree yielding fruit as in free surrender, but of thorns and thistles to be subdued by the sweat of man's brow. It speaks too of woman conceiving in sorrow and bearing in pain.

This is the poetry of ambiguity, reflecting the ambiguity in experience, in fact. The religious man, seeing what all men see, and at one with them in the suffering as in the satisfactions of life, asks *why* these things are, and gives his answer in terms of his religion, his apprehension of God. It follows that, whoever gave to these myths their literary forms, there lies behind them an awareness of, and a belief in, a God of a sort who would do these things: who would create a good world and take pleasure in its goodness; who would give man dominion and moral responsibility; who would inextricably link created harmony with a harmony of will, or freely chosen obedience; who would provide a way of redeeming the curse of disharmony and disobedience through the acceptance of toil, and of thorns and sweat upon a man's brow. The early chapters of Genesis are a product of this belief. The belief itself we owe to the great Hebrew prophets of the eighth to the sixth centuries B.C., to Amos, Hosea, Isaiah First and Second, Jeremiah, and Ezekiel. They it was who tied inextricably into one bundle the concepts of God, of creation, and of personal, social, and political morality. They it was who bound up in one religious nexus the human capacities to worship, to associate on a moral basis, to procreate, and to work. For them the practice of religion, the creation of a social order, the fulfilment of human sexuality, and the economic obligation of work were all of personal concern to God. To him, men were answerable for them all. Infidelity at any one point brought disorder into them all. The God who was Creator of the heaven and the earth was a faithful God: one who loved righteousness, or faithful dealing, and mercy, and dealt so with men; and one who willed, therefore, that they should deal so with one another. Work, from being a mere economic necessity, from being a curse occasioned by the hostility of the natural world, became a religious obligation and, when so accepted, a blessing from God for which man would respond appropriately in worship. For work, the work of the man in the field and of the woman bearing and nurturing her children, had become a partaking in the creative and the procreative work of God.

This witness of the Old Testament to a religious concept of work is continued in the New. "My Father worketh hitherto, and I work", said Jesus—enigmatically as ever (John v, 17). If, as the theologian would say, the mission of Jesus was to reveal, in the terms of a fully human life, all that God *can* reveal of himself, and to do, subject to the ultimate human limitation—the capacity to be done to death—all that man *can* do of the will of God, then this enigmatic saying is of profound significance for a theological view of work. It implies a participation in the blessing of creation and in redemption from the curse. Redemption was seen, in the old religious symbols, to be by way of the thorns and the sweat on the brow. The work of Jesus led him along that way (Matthew xxvii, 29, etc.; Luke xxii, 44). Christian theology sees in the work of Christ something redemptive done, objectively, for man. It sees also in men's work a grace, or privilege, or capacity, given by God enabling men to participate in this redemptive work of Christ. The participation may be—at its simplest—on the material level, in such use, both charitable and just, of the product of work as will enable the poor, the unprovided for, the deprived, to live—ideally, to create a living for themselves. The participation may be on the social level, enabling man to identify himself totally with his neighbour, and so to recognize their common humanity, their solidarity in good and ill. Without this identification there cannot be the third, and deepest, level of participation in the redemptive work of Christ—this which is given, not to all men, but only to those who can bear it: it is a spiritual participation, in which man both works and suffers, accepting deprivation and loss, consciously identifying it with the work of Christ, and so offering it vicariously with him. There are few who understand this inwardly; the writer of this essay is not among the few; but that it is a reality in the theological tradition he has no doubt, and he would be unfaithful were he not to record it. Yet it is also exhibited, symbolically, to many, week by week, day by day: for when the bread and the wine are offered in remembrance of the cross and resurrection of Jesus, in the Eucharist, the Holy Communion, the Mass, this participation of working man in the redeeming work of Christ is one among the truths there effectively symbolized.

The theologian's first concern is with Christian understanding, and so after that with what Christians actually do, or fail to do. As early as in two of St Paul's earliest epistles, those to the Thessalonians—that is, about A.D. 50 to 51—we find Christians reproved for being work-shy (1 Thessalonians iv, 11, v, 14; 2 Thessalonians iii, 6 ff). To live in idleness, St Paul says, is "not in accordance with the tradition" which they had received from him, or which, indeed, he had exemplified among them in his insistence on earning his own living, "with toil and labour working night and day". "If any will not work, neither let him eat," he had said when first instructing them in the Christian life. Not in idleness would the Christian community be established or the needs of the world be served.

It is on this basis that the Christian theology of work has been, traditionally, translated into practice. The very idea of 'the Christian life' presupposes participation in community: the notion that it is something particular to a man to which he has to bear individual witness in an alien or indifferent world is, though perhaps an inevitable and necessary corollary in the modern world, nevertheless a corollary originating in the modern world. The traditional concept is of a community in which either normative Christian relationships are given institutional form or fundamental human relationships are given Christian significance—the distinction is too subtle to be argued here—and in which there is developed that pattern of expectations and fulfilment which we call Christian ethics or the Christian way of life. In this, work, with its attendant disciplines, sanctions, and satisfactions, has its part. The products of work provide the economic support of the community, as the processes of work dictate, at least in part, its social organization and shape. On the product of the community, its wealth, there were, traditionally, two inalienable claims. One was provision for the worship of God, which had resulted in that Christian architecture, liturgical literature, and music which are now part of our culture. The other was provision for 'the poor', which has resulted in the entrenching of a notion of social obligation in the philosophy underlying modern society.

The actual social unit in which this notion of 'community', with its attendant life, became embodied has varied from century to century and from place to place. For long it was the monastic community, in its various shapes. In medieval times it was, co-existing with the monasteries, the socio-economic unit of manorial village or market town, also religiously conceived. From the time of the Reformation, with the temporary abandonment of the monastic life by Protestant Europe and the growth of towns beyond their earlier visible confines, the unit became more and more the household, within which the family unit formed part. Despite the changes, the double claim of 'God' and 'the poor' continued to be both made and acknowledged. Inevitably the claim of 'God' was both made and met with weakening force as what is now called secularization proceeded in the centuries since the Reformation. Inevitably the claim of 'the poor' was one which, more and more, could not be met, for since the sixteenth century the social and economic changes which have produced the modern industrialized, capitalistic society produced also new and much more extensive classes of 'poor', while it failed to produce a social organization adequate to deal with them. In this, post-Reformation theology showed its worst failure to develop. That its gospel of hard work and thrift contributed to the rise of modern capitalism has now become axiomatic; that it continued to articulate, in the name of God, the claims of 'the poor' can be proved from liturgy, library, and sermons. What it failed to do was to develop a theology of society which would utter some imperatives for the social and economic order itself, on the development and financing of the new industrial process; on the organization of men, and women and children, for work in the new industrial units; on the planning of towns and the provision of housing, education, hospitals, even churches, and all that we mean by social and community life suitable for the new pattern of work which the industrial revolution, in its several waves, brought upon Western Europe. In Victorian England F. D. Maurice, Charles Kingsley, J. M. Ludlow, and their associates were doing a new thing when they claimed the actual conditions of work and living in the slums of England as a proper concern of Christian theology, and when, in terms of what for a short time they called "Christian Socialism", they essayed some positive policies for reform. Since Maurice the Christian witness has been maintained, though—it must be confessed—sometimes more in anxiety than in achievement.[2] Today new changes are upon us, and attention to them must replace any regretful backward-looking towards the old.

The changes result from the application of modern technological developments, notably the computer, not only to the processes of work, but also to the organization of it and to the whole economy of production and distribution of the product.

The changes extend to agriculture as much as to the manufacturing industries: the policies of the EEC, for instance, will, if implemented, result in the reduction of the agricultural workforce in the EEC countries by eight million persons over the next few years. The mines will be further mechanized and, as natural gas and nuclear energy are developed, more and more mines will be closed[3]. In many branches of industry many men and women will have to leave what have become their settled occupations, move to another district, and learn new skills. If they do not or cannot move, if they do not or cannot learn, they will become 'redundant' in the most hopeless sense of that term.

It follows that the theological imperatives must change also if theology is to do its proper work. They must be directed no longer, exclusively, to the individual, as concerning personal moral choices and decisions within his personal control: to the employer, for instance, on providing just wages and proper conditions for his workman; to the lady, on how to treat her maid; or to all who 'have', enjoining a simple duty of charity to those who 'have not'. The imperatives must now be directed to those who plan and will control the new economy and the new social organization which will accompany it. They must be directed to those skilled in research in its many branches, requiring of them the most thorough assessment of how the new ways will impinge on men, what effects the new industrial processes will have upon men's lives. Together the planners and researchers must give to the rest of us some clear picture of the ends and consequences of what they do and propose to do. If they promise us increased wealth, together we must decide what to do with it: how the rewards of work are to be distributed between those engaged in it; how much of the gross product is to be given away, or released on very generous terms, to enable the capital development of underdeveloped countries and to enable them to trade.[4] We must decide what our priorities shall be in public expenditure at home—whether to renew the decayed heart of our older industrial towns and cities, and the educational and social provisions now so woefully inadequate in them;[5] or to renew hospitals and re-equip the health service; or to develop systems of public transport efficient and attractive enough to reduce the amount of unnecessary private motoring on our congested roads. Merely to create wealth, without responsible planning for the right use of it, would be to forget the end for which work and wealth exist, which is to serve the common good of men and to create such conditions as will help them to live, together, the good life.

The same application of mind, and the harnessing of a corporate will, must be directed to 'redundancy'.[6] To change work may require a man to move home—that is, to uproot a family from among its friends and associations and the children from their school. It takes time for the anonymities of urban life to yield to the formation of satisfying friendships and the forms of free association which a settled life normally require. Even church congregations are sometimes harder to join than to leave. These are the intangible aspects of the upheaval which a change of work may demand; add these to the problem of finding a house and setting up home and the demand is high. To help to accommodate themselves to change of this sort requires a community undertaking which has hardly yet begun. It requires the pooling of local resources of social knowledge and skill together with the goodwill and spirit of service which ought to be coming from the churches and from other community-minded groups.

The social problems are far greater for immigrant peoples from overseas, from climates and cultures very different from our own. To achieve a harmonious solution of these is, without doubt, the most pressing domestic task facing Britain today. A special number of *Crucible*, the Journal of the Church Assembly Board for Social Responsibility, published in May 1965, assessed some aspects of the problem and described the initiatives being taken to resolve it[7]; more work has been done since then under the auspices of the Committee for Commonwealth Immigrants and of the Institute of Race Relations; Continental Europe has a similar task in securing good conditions of life and work for migrants from Mediterranean countries who come to work in the industries of the north. The EEC, the International Union of Family Organizations, and other bodies are properly engaged upon this.

The last few paragraphs have been occupied with an indication—no more—of some of the social problems arising from changing conditions of work today. Very considerable efforts are being made to understand these problems, and to meet them by efficient administrative means. Why is this? There are sound, economic, social, and political reasons why such measures should be taken, and should succeed. In hard, materialist terms there will be trouble if they do not: production will suffer, the economic organization will not run efficiently, there will be social and political troubles which it would be costly to subdue. But this is not the whole answer. Behind these materialist answers there lies a conviction about men, about their intrinsic worth, about their right to be protected in the enjoyment of certain liberties, about their value, not as workers but as men. This conviction has a theological foundation, in a belief about God and about man made in the image and likeness of God, however much it may now be forgotten. But, the conviction having been established, and become part of a general humane or humanitarian concern, why not leave it there, without bringing in theology at all?

The answer must be No. It is fashionable to speak now of 'the autonomy of the secular world', to claim that at all levels, including that of human organization, it runs according to the internal logic of its own processes which are not open to religious interpretation or influence; it runs as though without God. There are Christians who hail this belief as liberation, as an advance. But the notion of autonomy can work both ways. The internal logic of technological and administrative processes—like any other logic—can become a tyrant, a prison, the very devil. These words were written on a day when two things were in the news. It was announced that the number of unemployed in Britain was the highest in the month of July for any year since 1940—the first year of the Second World War—and this despite a quarter of a century of social, political, and economic planning more concentrated than ever before in our history. The will to reduce unemployment is general; yet, such is the 'autonomy' of the country's economic life, the figure will not stay down.[8] On the same day London heard the last of a series of experimental 'sonic booms', designed by the Ministry of Technology to test the public reaction to but a little of the noise which will become an inescapable part of life once supersonic aircraft go into regular commercial use. No-one was deceived by the epithet 'experimental' attached to these tests: whatever the public reaction, there will be sonic booms. The Concorde aircraft has made its test flight, and seventy or so of such aircraft are already on order. The aircraft is being built, not to meet an overwhelming public demand to fly to another continent in a little less time, but in obedience to an internal logic, that of the aircraft industry. Supersonic flight is technically possible; there are prestige and money to be earned in developing it—and in being the first; England and France must therefore develop it before the U.S.A. does so. The Minister of Technology has said in the House of Commons that to forbid supersonic over-flying would be to turn away orders for the aircraft. The autonomy of the politico-economic process will not be overthrown by arguments from a consideration of general amenity or of prior moral claims upon not unlimited sources.[9]

The Concorde project is not instanced in order to condemn technological advance in the name of theology. It is to demonstrate the claim that 'autonomy' in any sector of life can jeopardize the rest of it; that, in the name of the whole, the autonomy of the part must be kept within bounds. When technologists begin to say, "It can happen; therefore it must", theologians are bound to reply, "It need not happen: the need has to be proved"; or, "It may not happen, unless there is no better way of avoiding a specific ill"; or even, "It must not happen at all: thou shalt not". But before he utters this prohibition the theologian must be sure of his ground. Happily, with regard to technological development in general, he has no need to take any such negative stand. On the contrary, the theologian can welcome it as an extension of the means of man's dominion which the Book of Genesis described as God's first blessing to mankind. The fulness of the Christian vision of this has been aptly summarized in some very condensed sentences by Dr Hugo Meynell of the University of Leeds:

Once we have some preliminary idea of the Gospel as having some objective content, and of Christian ethics as derived from beliefs about the ultimate fate of man in the next world as well as in this one, a genuine attempt can be made at a *rapprochement* between the Christian doctrine of man and the rational appraisal of his place within contemporary industrial society. Genesis, chapter 1, vv. 26–27, describes God's decree that men should be in command of the earth and all the creatures that are in it. Twentieth-century man has perhaps come to maturity at least in the sense that in him, for the first time in history, this promise is realized. Man is brought into partnership with God in the bringing about of a new world and of a new society within that world.

The direction of Christian hope towards the future within a redeemed world, and not a heaven which is simply apart from this material world, is something which is both profoundly biblical and implicit in Christian tradition (in the doctrine of the resurrection of the body), and coherent with the knowledge of industrial man that he himself is transforming the material world. What is really new in this conception is that God seems to be using men as his instrument in the re-creation of the world. That God both uses worldly instruments and himself transcends them, that we are secondary causes within his primary causality, as the scholastics would say, is, of course, a very old Christian and Old Testament doctrine. But to believe it sincerely is to be saved both from the despair that all human work is ultimately vain which emphasizes too much God's transcendence and distance from man), and from the presumption that man is able entirely of himself to propose his own ideals and dispose of his own fate: Man's dignity and limitation is as an instrument of God's purposes, alone as he is among the material creation, as St Thomas Aquinas notes, in being a *free* instrument. Only with the growth of technology does it begin to appear how it is that man reconciled to God in Christ may be God's secondary cause in the re-creation of the world. Only now, perhaps, can we begin to understand the full meaning of the astonishing Pauline phrase, "co-workers with God".[10]

Let there be, however, no illusion about what technological development of itself can do. It may give the world more and a greater range of industrial products, with less toil, less sheer drudgery, for more men. It may give some men more leisure—more than they will know what to do with, unless our methods of education succeed more in captivating the imagination. But there is little prospect yet of its leaving many others less busy than they were before, for their work is of a sort which cannot be mechanized. The human race differs from all other species in the high proportion of the life span which must be given to the rearing of its young, to the imparting of learned skills and behaviour. As society becomes more complex this period of dependence, of being educated, grows longer. Neither do the strains of life grow less. Some physical diseases and modes of suffering have been checked, some almost eliminated; but others, like injury on the road and disease from stress and from radiation, have taken their place. Psychological and spiritual strain are either increasing or are more readily recognized, less masked by other ills or less firmly controlled by internal powers. There is no indication that these strains will be less in the new technological age. It follows, therefore, that the promise of a new era of leisure with plenty is a closely qualified promise. Professional people, particularly those in the healing, caring, teaching, and thinking professions, see little prospect of more leisure but rather of less. For them work, hard and long, is still a condition of vocation, for which society promises little in terms of comparative reward. A theology of work must assert the obligation of a just reward. It must assert also the freedom to find satisfaction in the work, as well as in the reward. And it must assert that the end of work is rest, contemplation, or, in the old Christian word, fruition—which is enjoyment. The eyes which today are fixed upon the wheel are focused also for an eternal vision of God.

¹ See Michael Harrington, *The Other America* (Penguin Books, 1963). See also L. Richard Hoffmann, "Automation and the Community", and Ian Smith, "Cybernation and the Ministry of the Church", in *Crucible* (London, Church Information Office, November 1966).

² See M. B. Reckitt, *Maurice to Temple: A Century of the Social Movement in the Church of England* (1947); and the standard biographies of, and monographs upon, and works by F. D. Maurice, Charles Kingsley, J. M. Ludlow, Henry Scott Holland, B. F. Westcott, Charles Gore, C. E. Raven, William Temple; see also *Christendom* and other works of the Christendom Group; the C.O.P.E.C. Reports; and *Crucible* (Church Information Office, since 1962).

³ Lord Robens, Chairman of the National Coal Board, estimated "that manpower in the [mining] industry would fall by more than 300,000, to one-sixth of its present size in the next twelve years, if the Government's present policies were pursued", leaving a work force of only 65,000 (*The Times*, November 11th and 13th, 1967). The closure of 70 to 75 pits, planned for the year April 1968 to March 1969, would make 17,000 men redundant; by 1970–71 the decrease in man-power would be at the rate of 35,000 a year (*The Times*, reporting a White Paper on fuel policy, May 6th, 1968).

⁴ See *The Family in Contemporary Society* (SPCK, 1958), pp. 9–11, 154 ff, 161 ff. René Dumont and Bernard Rosier, *Nous allons à la Famine* (Paris: Ed. du Seuil, 1966). "Towards Starvation", *The Times Literary Supplement*, August 17th, 1967. "Overcoming Apathy in Development Aid", *The Times Business News*, November 4th, 1968.

⁵ See The Newsom Report, *Half our Future* (HMSO, 1964), and
K. R. Gray, "Nothing by Halves" (*Crucible*, July 1964).

⁶ See Sir Leon Bagrit, *The Age of Automation* (Reith Lectures, 1965);
Simon Phipps, "Automation and Ethics" (*Crucible*, November 1965);
and Hilda R. Kahn, "Uses and Abuses of Redundancy" (*Crucible*,
March 1967).

⁷ Of the voluminous more recent literature, see especially Jeremiah
Newman, *Race: Migration and Integration* (London, Burns and Oates,
1968).

⁸ By August 25th the figure had risen by a further 58,006 to 555,081
unemployed, and a total of 750,000 or more—2·6 per cent of the work
force—was forecast for the mid-winter months, even without bad
weather (*The Times*, August 25th, 1967). By early November government spokesmen were defending themselves against the charge of
requiring a pool of unemployment as an instrument of economic
policy by emphasizing 're-deployment' as their long-term intention,
towards which a period of unemployment was a transitory step. After
a slight fall in the spring of 1969, the August total of unemployed reached
a new peak of 567,828, the highest August figure since 1940 (*The Times
Business News*, March 21st, May 23rd, June 20th, August 21st, 1969).
A headline in the same paper, April 23rd, 1968, points to the ambiguity
of 'autonomy': "Unemployment Rise Puzzles the Analysts." Official
efforts are now directed less to the abolition of unemployment than to
"Easing the Impact of Redundancy" (*Ibid.*, August 18th, 1969).

⁹ The estimated cost of the Concorde in 1962 was £150,000,000–
£170,000,000; in May 1969 it was £730,000,000, with the possibility of
further rises envisaged. The Committee of Public Accounts commented
adversely on the lack of control over such escalating expenditure. It
was stated in evidence to the Committee that the passenger payload
represented only "a tiny fraction"—6 per cent—of the overall weight
(*The Times*, August 2nd, 1967; August 14th, 1969).

¹⁰ "Notes towards a Theology of Man in Industry" (*Crucible*, The
Journal of the Church Assembly Board for Social Responsibility, March
1966, p. 36). Reprinted in *The New Theology and Modern Theologians*
(Sheed and Ward, 1967), Chapter 5. See also Alan Nicholson, *The
Biblical Doctrine of Work* (S.C.W. Press, 1958).

12 | *The Business of Business*

by ANDREW ROBERTSON

Andrew Robertson was a research officer on the staff of the National Institute of Economic and Social Research, and is now with the Science Policy Research Unit at the University of Sussex. Formerly he was Head of Publications Division at the British Institute of Management and Editor of *The Manager*, having been an industrial correspondent of *The Times*.

He has edited the *Penguin Survey of Business and Industry*, has written a short history of the trade unions, and has collaborated on *A Guide to Industrial Relations* with Leonard Neal. With his wife, Jean, he contributes a weekly column to the *New Statesman* on consumer affairs.

Someone said somewhere that the business of business is business, and if that sounds American it may be because in the United States businessmen and their critics and advisers have wrestled more energetically with the problem of values, or ethics, or objectives, in business than in any other industrial society. They have achieved a high level of prosperity, be it uneven to the point of instability, and they have achieved it through largely private enterprise. Therefore at the peak of their material achievement it is not unnatural for their leaders to take stock of what has been done, and ask themselves and their fellows whether they have achieved what they all really want. That is what the Good Society means in essence. That is what Professor Galbraith is referring to in *The New Industrial State* when he says in an addendum on economic method: "The espousal of non-economic goals has an aspect of menace from which the professionally sensitive automatically recoil. They dismiss such extra-economic concerns as 'soft', which is to say that they are professionally substandard".

Elsewhere we have read that the sign of business success is a continual rise in profits, because thus the enterprise becomes less vulnerable. Hence the anxiety with which businesses seek

annually to better the profit margins of yesteryear. This is not
the place to discuss the methods by which such arithmetical
successes may be scored (and there is an element of self-
delusion in the chase after short-term gains of this nature), but
on the face of it there are two comments to be made about the
relations between profit and other corporate objectives. The
first is that the adoption of seemingly altruistic objectives
(such as shorter hours for child workers or a lower accident rate)
may eventually redound to the further prosperity of the enterprise. Robert Owen added that telling argument to his address
To the British Master Manufacturers.

> A very limited share of sagacity, properly directed, will
> show us that, in our character of manufacturers only, it is
> clearly our interest to permit children to be properly educated,
> and to possess sound and vigorous constitutions;—that our
> operatives and all the working classes should not be asked
> or permitted to labour more than twelve hours per day, with
> two hours' intermission, for rest, air, and meals, and that, in
> return for their labour, they should be allowed wages suffi-
> cient to purchase wholesome food and some of the most useful
> articles of manufacture.

The quotation is worth its full length for the detail, for the
implicit message that the conditions listed were not allowed to
the operatives of Owen's fellow-manufacturers. And, of course,
most of them did not respond to his plea, because they did not
believe that it would be to their material advantage, on the contrary. Nor did they care to consider whether their scale of
values was in some other sense wrong. Which is the second
point regarding 'non-economic goals' or unbusinesslike objectives. That where they do not appear to promise eventual, or
long-term, economic advantages they are apt not to be pursued.
Hence the conflict.

There is an interesting proposition of Spinoza's, Proposition
XXXI in the fourth part of his *Ethics*, that may be relevant to
this second consideration, if we assume that apparently non-
economic goals may in the long run prove to be advantageous
or disadvantageous to the enterprise, and therefore, paradoxically, assume an economic importance not at first sight obvious.
It reads: "In so far as anything agrees with our nature, thus
far it is necessarily good." The proof lies in the realization that
whatever agrees with our nature cannot be bad, but must

either be good or indifferent. If the latter, we are faced with the absurd conclusion that nothing can follow from an agreeable effect on our nature.

To clarify this simple but obscurely phrased proposition in concrete terms, take such profit-making activities as open-cast mining, chemical manufacture, metal manufacture, underground mining, atomic-power supply (assumed to be profitable), and any other such activity that has a direct impact upon the community in the short or long term. Open-cast mining will be less profitable if the topsoil and vegetation are reinstated after the ores have been recovered. Therefore in many cases they have not been, and the land has been left for others to deal with as they may. It may be several generations before the community or the nation comes to look upon the man-made wilderness that open-cast workings leave as, in Spinoza's words, "contrary to that which agrees with our nature". But, natural or unnatural, a wilderness is a waste of resources, and in our hypothetical case became so as an incidental consequence of the short-term maximization of profits by one particular business unit. It follows, within the limits of this example, that the relationship between profits, or business success which they purport to measure, and non-economic objectives may be more intricate and less easily discerned than we always realize.

It has, not surprisingly, taken a long time to arrive at this understanding, because we have first to look back at the chain of events that led, say, from the setting up of a dyeworks on the banks of a trout stream to the sterilization of the stream, the eventual disappearance of natural life from its environment, and the eventual abandonment of the works in favour of a better site with more abundant water, leaving an unusable empty shell, of interest only to industrial archaeologists, and another man-made wilderness. Only when the consequential losses can be measured or observed can we make any estimate of the true cost of such an undertaking. It is not a cost of the kind that enters either into the calculations of company accountants or finds itself included in the aggregates dealt in by theoretical economists. For one simple reason is that *prima facie* it is not a cost that can be taken into account by the business.

Most industrial societies have had to hedge their entrepreneurs round with restrictions in order to avoid this kind of long-run social cost, and often they have been too late. Most industrial societies, in addition, have had to pass through a philosophical phase that prevented restraints being placed upon economic activity—the phase of unqualified belief in free and unrestricted private enterprise. The classical statement of this mode of thought is found in Adam Smith:

> The natural effort of every individual to better his own condition, when suffered to exert itself with freedom and security, is so powerful a principle, that it is alone, and without any assistance, not only capable of carrying on the society to wealth and prosperity, but of surmounting a hundred impertinent obstructions with which the folly of human laws too often incumbers its operations.

Professor Howard Bowen, in *Social Responsibilities of the Businessman*, published in 1953 in the United States, reminded his readers that such a *laissez-faire* principle did not exclude certain moral rules which were largely taken for granted by the businessman of the day, such as the preservation of private property, the observance of contracts, and the avoidance of deception and fraud.

Some of the restraints to which Adam Smith refers when he polemizes that the greatest praise of a statesman would be "that he discovered error and removed it; that he found a country harassed by restrictions and regulations, and that he freed it", were not necessarily aimed at the balancing of profit-seeking activity by protective legislation for the community at large. Sometimes they were (an old and unsuccessful example was the Elizabethan Statute of Artificers, which worked no better than its numerous predecessors and fell into disuse long before repeal). At other times they were intended to compel the businessman to share his prosperity with the Government of the day, and perhaps the community at large might benefit from that, and perhaps not. There were other restrictions imposed upon him that derived from the desire of his competitors to secure themselves from his 'unfair' practices, such as monopolizing sources of raw material. During the period of Smith's greatest influence over men's minds Governments were urged, and were sometimes in the mood, to disembarrass business of unnecessary hindrances. The battles were all joined, therefore, around the standard of what was deemed to be 'necessary'.

Peter Drucker, writing in *The New Society* back in 1951, said that "Archangels in command of an industrial enterprise would have to make profitability as much the first law of their actions and policies as the greediest 'capitalist'. And so must the most faithful Commissar . . ." He extends the proposition to the point where the individual entrepreneur's desire for profit (the greedy capitalist, with or without quotation marks) is irrelevant, for the justification of profit is merely "the objective necessity and purpose of industrial production and industrial economy". Thus reassured, we know where the priorities lie. First make your profits so that your enterprise may survive and prosper (how this is divorced from the gains of the individuals who head the enterprise is unclear, but the message is simple otherwise). Then, when the position is secure, attention may be turned to other aspects of responsibility.

Drucker is, of course, right. Without its corporate income, profit, to be used for growth, for the reward for risk-bearing investors and the directors and managers, there would be no enterprise. Whether a particular enterprise needs to continue its existence at all depends on its nature and on our collective attitude to it. Society has made certain rules about that, and there are enterprises, such as smuggling syndicates, which it will not tolerate, at least not always and not in most countries. It becomes much more difficult to evaluate the activities of a business in social or moral terms if it is not actually infringing some clear and definite laws. At one time, and even now here and there, some people would have said that drink and tobacco manufacture were undesirable. Others would have condemned armament manufacture. And still others the making of birth-control devices.

The product of the firm, therefore, does matter in the scale of values, not merely of society at large, but of the people involved in the enterprise. One of the best-known sources of poor morale among employees of a company is the realization that they are working for a dubious, perhaps unscrupulous, money-grabbing concern. The poor morale does not take the form of labour disputes, generally, but a more subtle resistance to the firm in the form of time-wasting, poor work, and even pilfering. It is a curious fact that none of the writers on industrial psychology pays attention to the phenomenon of dishonesty in the firm as a symptom of antagonism to the enterprise and what it stands for. The management itself is inclined to dismiss it, along with its perpetrators, as yet another instance of the general deterioration of social standards. But it could be, and often is, a sickness particular to that firm in those circumstances. It is not a security officer that is needed then, but a new corporate philosophy.

While, therefore, it would be useless to argue that profit was not pre-eminent in the priorities of a business, it does not follow that profit justifies the activities of that business. Regardless of the nature of the product or service that is provided for payment in the expectation of eventual profit, a business may deceive its customers by making false claims about its product, by misleading advertising, or by pretending that the value of the product is greater than it is. If these phenomena were uncommon there would have been no need for protective legislation such as industrial countries are now contemplating or bringing into force. Here it is the firm's customers who are being maltreated, and some would argue that this is a short-sighted policy because it will eventually alienate them and damage the business. Again, economic self-interest seems to militate against sharp business practice. But it is extraordinary how few businessmen struggling for survival in a competitive situation are prepared to see that far ahead and prefer to believe with P. T. Barnum that "There's one born every minute", and to take the idea a step further and exploit these implicitly innocent individuals.

There seems to be, therefore, a distinct difference between the lot of the shareholder and the lot of the customer, as far as the profit-making enterprise is concerned. The businessman or manager's duty towards the shareholder is clear and can even be made to seem precise. He must be rewarded. However, it has not been unusual in recent years, and particularly since the coming of limited liability, for investors to be treated as ruthlessly as casual customers, individuals to be fleeced as quickly and effectively as possible.

The third group of people upon whom the enterprise has had a similar impact in the past is different, in that it was and still is collectively not susceptible of being fleeced of its money like the investor or the customer. The employee possesses something else that the enterprise needs, labour, and sometimes skill. The most cursory reading of social history in industrial countries shows that for a long time (as the quotation from Owen implied) employers took a short-term view of their relationship with working people. To put it briefly and brutally, they were to be used to the limit of their physical endurance, and then discarded. Anyone nice-minded enough to doubt this should study the disillusionment of the early factory inspectors, and especially Leonard Horner, who began by assuming that mill-owners were reasonable men open to be educated in the purpose of the laws to protect young people, and ended by prosecuting them. The conspiracies of evasion and chicanery resorted to by men of substance and standing in order to cheat a well-intentioned and publicly approved set of regulations illustrate the subordination of one set of values to another at that stage of industrial development. It is arguable that, in this country at least, and probably in a number of others, industrial society is still paying some of the price for this preoccupation with what has proved to be short-term material gain.

To come up to date, we have to face the fact that the regulation of businessmen is now a part of our legal structure precisely because they have in the past abused their undoubted power. They are not the only social group to have done so, but while the repercussions of their activities were not fully understood serious damage was being done, not only to the physical amenities and material resources of nations, but to the social fabric. The Americans, who have studied this question more closely than any other nation, are able to describe the reaction of businessmen to State regulation in such terms as these: "While regulation came to businessmen with a relatively low price tag, it nevertheless was burdensome and exacted a toll of anxiety, frustration, and dejection beyond all relation to the economic cost." (Lane, *The Regulation of Businessmen*, 1966.)

Robert Lane, the author of this Yale University study, explains that the reason for this down-in-the-mouth response to legitimate State control was that the rules "challenged the businessman's belief system, profaned his idols and depreciated his myths". Furthermore, it appeared to lower his status in the community, it denigrated him and attacked his 'business ego'. Worst still, it hampered his freedom of decision, to which he had become accustomed, and added to the uncertainties that normally beset any business. All this is perfectly understandable. Indeed, psychologists like Karen Horney and Gordon

Allport have recorded their view that the hostility evinced by one-time 'free agents' to regulation is in part a reaction to induced uncertainty and anxiety.

C. Wright Mills in *The Power Elite* concentrated more on the pecuniary standard. What urges men on to do things that might be considered unethical, even immoral, in business is the pursuit of money. "Whenever the standards of moneyed life prevail, the man with money, no matter how he got it, will eventually be respected." That is a difficult assertion to deny because the word 'eventually' can mean a very long time indeed. But Professor Mills develops the point by adding that in any society where the pursuit of money "is the commanding value in relation to which the influence of other values had declined, so men easily become morally ruthless in the pursuit of easy money and fast estate-building". Mills is, in fact, also concerned with out-and-out corruption in business, and only the very innocent would try to pretend that industrial society has not seen quite a lot of that, from the suddenly fashionable industrial espionage (the Lombe brothers were accused of it in the eighteenth century) to the private deals with public officials that now and again reach the courts.

It does seem, on the face of it, as if Professor Bowen were being too flattering in his assumption, cited above, that whatever freedom men in business exercise they still tend to conform to a basic moral code. Some, perhaps a majority, would. Some business communities, like the City of London, have prospered as a result of being widely reputed for keeping verbal commitments. Nevertheless, careful though the institutions that make up the City may be, there are still the few who require to be disciplined by them for breaches of the ethical code. To say this, and the knowledgeable will put upon it the weight it deserves, is merely to bring to light the fact that the pressures of business are capable of sweeping aside most men's scruples. It has to be added that now and again there seems to appear on the business scene an individual or two who possess no scruples whatever.

If, therefore, the pressures of business are forceful enough to bring businessmen into conflict with each other and with the State in the formation of which they play an important part we should not be surprised if, unregulated, businessmen focus their attention on the profitability of their business at the expense of sections of the community or of the community as a whole. So, archangel or 'greedy capitalist' at its head, the profitability and survival of the business entity will be put first. Taking issue with Dr Drucker (and it may be that he would not write that sentence today that was quoted earlier), it must be said that if by archangel he meant to suggest, as he doubtless did, a highly moral person, it is conceivable that such a man might be prepared to forgo profit in favour of conscience. But, as Mills would contend, and Galbraith would support him, that would not be looked upon as 'practical' by his fellow-directors.

Values in business and industry must therefore be considered always in the shadows of the money-motive, individual and collective. To turn the earlier idea round, it would be decidedly impractical to do otherwise. This may leave out of account a preoccupation of big business when it has arrived at a size and profitability (perhaps from monopolistic advantages) that allows it to consider 'non-economic' matters. That preoccupation is with its 'corporate image' or its public relations. It is at this stage that values come under scrutiny because it becomes possible to be freer in taking them into account. The cynical would comment that at this stage it must be too late to turn altruistic, but that is not necessarily true. For one thing it puts the big business in the position of exemplar and will have some effect on standards and values generally. That can only be advantageous for the community at large.

But business being evolutionary and comprised of many more smaller enterprises striving to grow and prosper than large, successful companies consolidating their position by earning goodwill, the prevalent ethics of the majority will still need regulation and supervision. Not every profit-seeking entrepreneur, even in these enlightened times, can see the long-run gains to be had from doing as you would be done by.

I 3 | *Vocation and Industry*

by THE VERY REV. ROBIN WOODS

Robin Woods was educated at Gresham's School, Holt, and at Trinity College, Cambridge. He joined the staff of the Student Christian Movement and worked primarily amongst the colleges of London, and during the early years of the War in Birmingham and Nottingham. After military service as a Chaplain he became vicar of the industrial parish of South Wigston, Leicester (where he shared in the beginnings of Inter-Church Consultations with Management and Trade Unions).

He was appointed Archdeacon of Singapore in 1951, where he shared in the planning and the work of the Church in South-east Asia. (Throughout the emergency in Malaya and for some further years his main work was in building up the English-speaking Chinese Church in the area.)

Before his present appointment he was Archdeacon of Sheffield from 1958, and it was during these years that he was able to share in the close contact established between the Church and industry that was so unique in the Diocese of Sheffield. Since his appointment as Dean of Windsor in 1962 Robin Woods had the conviction that St George's Chapel should exercise a wider ministry in the realm of consultation and teaching. St George's House was opened in October 1966 as a direct result of his conviction that there should be a centre where Church and State could meet for dialogue and discussion on a wide range of issues.

In a discussion in the Sixth Form of a grammar school it was said to me, "At least you had your minds made up for you when you were conscripted and went to war! And that meant going places." The words were spoken not in jealousy or in hopes of a further emergency in which to serve, but with the wistful thought that to make one's own decision of what to do was nearly impossible, and if a decision was reached it brought with it little prospect of using insight or courage. Yet freedom in one's home, freedom in choice of work, freedom to work and try out other avenues is a basic foundation of our society: it is a quality of the capitalist system which, more than anything else, justifies the social structure of our society. Freedom of choice is that which basically distinguishes ourselves from communist and other autocratic neighbours. Vocation is the responsible use of this freedom: vocation implies a calculated choice with a motive behind it. The will to work is basic to human nature to a greater or lesser extent; the vocation governing that work is the expression of an individual's personality within it.

Whereas the vocation to serve and develop one's own individual abilities is fairly easy to analyse if that vocation leads to one of the professions such as medicine, law, the Civil Service, or the ministry of the Church, it is by no means so easy to pinpoint the motives that lie behind the vocation to industry. Too often the way is open to industry as the line of least resistance or as a mode to work out one's rent for taking up space in the country. On a lower level industrial work is seen as something that can be abandoned at short notice, or as an escape from a wholly impersonal and anonymous world. The common view of industry taken by the vast majority of those leaving secondary modern schools is a place in which to earn money without incurring responsibility and with the expectation of quick returns and good pay-packets. This attitude has with the other motives mentioned led to a false evaluation of our industrial community as a responsible professional element of the highest importance in the life of our nation. If there was a more common intent to look for power and influence, then there would be less cause for anxiety, but men these days are not looking for power or responsibility: they are hoping for one element of power only: the power of money. The vocation to serve in industry with a degree of dedication that leads to long hours and unpaid overtime has sprung in the past from the grammar- and public-school tradition. For this reason alone any abandonment of this type of education bodes ill.

In the commercial and industrial context there can and must remain a real sense of duty first of all in what we might call the routine activities of industry; these include duty and payment to shareholders, to whom, only in the United Kingdom, boards are legally responsible, duty to consumers in matters of quality, and a wider duty to the nation. Vocation also shows itself in duty towards the suppliers of raw materials;

this stands out plainly in the case of the vegetable-oil, chocolate, jute, tea, rubber, and other industries. Others develop a vocation in industry along the well-worn tracks of industrial relations and personnel management. All these pursuits are proper to our industrial structure, and none should be denigrated in any way; they make up the ingredients of motivation and vocation. Yet circumstances deny the pioneering spirit today except for the determined few, and the call to serve and make industry a vocational career remains illusive.

Only a few years ago the colonial or imperial circumstances provided a memorable sphere in which sacrificial service was given in countless situations by those with a vocation to give it. This was most obviously true in Government, education, or the Church. Today such vocation has to be exercised not in Government or in the attitude of the 'haves' meeting the 'have-nots', but in the vocation to provide both at home and overseas. There is surely a social service in the agricultural and organic-chemical industries that are determined to provide sufficient protein and other essential food in the right proportion to the undernourished millions of Africa and Asia. There will also only be found sufficient clothing for the ragged, sufficient housing for the homeless, sufficient reading material for the newly literate if the vocation to provide is stimulated and developed. All too often it is economically unrewarding to open up factories or develop backward areas in such places as the Congo or Pakistan, and the decision to do so remains untaken, and the people of such areas degenerate in greater numbers and greater poverty. The decision to establish possibly uneconomic industries remains a matter for those with a vocation to do so and those with public funds to undergird it. No longer is it a case of good money or quick return by proceeding overseas; it is a case of public duty and individual calling.

The ready response shown in Voluntary Service Overseas is an indication that the post-war generation has a will to serve and to give. The fact that individuals recruited to work in international commercial enterprises such as Shell, Unilever, or the banks, are willing to undertake courses to learn the needs and outlooks of other territories and, when overseas, to share in multi-racial and multi-colour enterprises is an indication of the vocation to share our affluence and to extend the benefits of our civilization. But all these essential side activities go forward on an inner sense of vocation by the individual and a resolute determination to meet with and raise up the community to which he is sent. The preservation of dedication and vocation in these islands has in the past been curiously linked up with the readiness to serve overseas. Often by sending the best the long-term good of our country has been well served. The same is true of our new international and inter-racial age: it must not be served by the mediocre or money-making, but by men and women dedicated to a purpose. This is the only long-term answer to the colour and racial problems of today, and these are much bigger than any purely industrial issue. They will loom larger and larger before the eyes of Government, Church, and the community as a whole.

One might wish to develop in this collection of essays the pioneering element in vocation that meant so very much to our grandparents, and to a limited extent to our parents. It is, however, unrealistic to expect the bulk of those entering industry to share in such emotionally satisfying and highly creative jobs. The circumstances of the Industrial Revolution divided the life of the nation into what we may call the 'clean' professions and the 'dirty' industries. A veneer of sanctity was given to those who had a vocation to one of the professions, but no such aura was attached to those who went into industry. It is now plain that work in industry is as educationally, socially, and religiously important as work in the professions. It will, nevertheless, take time to develop a real sense of calling and vocational service in business. This sense of vocation will be discovered in the first instance through teamwork. The determination to work alongside others to the extent of sharing the monetary outcome is the beginning of teamwork, but it needs to be deeper than a group bonus added to basic wages: it finds its expression in trusting other people's judgments, in sharing in your colleagues' frustrations or failures, and in giving and receiving a deep-down confidence in the human nature of those who surround the work on hand. The greatness of the coal-mining industry has not only been born by sharing a common danger, it has been hammered out on the anvil of difficult and hard work overcome by a team spirit. This used to be true of the railway and transport industry: it is now a matter of re-discovering the vocation to work together and not in isolation, to work for a whole and not an isolated result. The challenge to the nationalized industries in creating a new community around coal, transport, steel, and whatever else is to be included, is a challenge to teamwork and group initiatives: these are vocations and not just employment. The contentment and good relations that have existed in the steel industry over the past twenty years were very impressive to one such as myself who lived and worked in Sheffield. At all levels, whether tending the furnaces, in the rolling mills, at the drawing-board, or in the offices, there has been built up a community commitment which is an immense asset to the steel trade. If the nationalization of the industry retains and extends this sense of commitment right through the industry, then, and then only, it will have been justified.

A man with a vocation and dedication often appears to work as a lone wolf, but in fact he finds it essential for survival to keep in close touch with his fellow-professionals or fellow-craftsman; by so doing he learns to recognize and work with his other allies in the same cause whoever they may be. In a rather similar fashion, at an early stage, the Church learnt to work through very small cells of a few individuals. They became the larger unit, but only after a prolonged period of learning to trust each other and find a common purpose.

Here is should be added that automation is not necessarily the cancellation of vocation. Sir Leon Bagrit began his Reith Lectures by saying:

> For many people, automation is a terrifying word. It conjures up visions of machines reducing man to the state of a mere pusher of buttons or watcher of dials, and abolishing the need for human thought and judgement. I can sympathize with those fears, but I am sure they are unjustified. We are not destined to become a race of babysitters for computers. Automation is not a devil, a Frankenstein. It is no more than a tool, but a tool of such immense possibilities that no one can yet see the full extent of what it might achieve for mankind.

It can readily be seen that automation, which is the installation of automatic machinery, and cybernetics, which is the control and planning of work processes, are rapidly taking shape in Britain. On the surface they appear damaging to personal freedom and individual initiative, but within this new structure the individual is not less but more important: it calls for not less but more intelligence, and for more understanding of one's colleagues on the job. The first automatic warehouse that will dispense 4000 different products to 1200 different outlets is now being built. Within such a place, or in any sphere where computer work speeds the activities of those who work, the individual finds he can never work alone; in management or on the shop floor his success lies in the lack of demarcation between the two and in the vocation to serve the whole. This lesson of non-demarcation particularly needs to be learnt by the trade unions.

Automation is being introduced in a piecemeal way, so the total effect is only gradual. It is true that new production methods and changing techniques set long experience and even craftmanship at a discount; the older worker may lose his importance and the younger one suffer from machine-tending, but overall the individual is being freed to be himself and is being liberated from ghastly monotony, thus enabling his personality to develop. The qualities obtained in the age of automation are the qualities of individual dedication and individual judgment, and at the same time opportunities for leisure that we in western civilization have not begun to appreciate.

If teamwork and the community of production form inaugural lines of vocation in the new industrial society, then a sense of individual responsibility forms the second avenue to explore. By responsibility we mean the ability and the determination to respond positively to each new situation as it arises, even the situation that seems like the stagnation of opportunity. Speaking of the required attributes of a man in an overseas appointment, Ann Boyd says, "He is required to be a man possessing high mobility, able to cope with rapid changes and to take whatever action may be necessary. He is therefore assumed to be highly responsible and autonomous even in situations of great stress, crisis, and temptation. Thoroughly pragmatic and profane, he is an A1 candidate for the world of the 'secular city'." This ability to stand alone, although this sounds like a contradiction to working together, is in fact quite consistent with our having to know how to work well with a very varied team of colleagues. A true employee works under authority, and he must be ready to take orders from his superiors, and yet he must be an inner-directed person, able to maintain a sense of direction when, in general, purposes and plans appear to be absent, able to convey a sense of purpose and, above all, of enthusiasm for the work on hand when such ingredients are in short supply. With a labour force that is becoming more and more mobile and with the sense of security in local labour being increasingly less, there is a call to be personally involved with one's colleagues and not just acquainted with them, to share their hopes and anxieties and not just to suffer them.

There should be added, in our communal and industrial activities, the call to excellence. In the ordinary sphere of safety, of working the Factory Acts, of the supervision of labour in the presence of danger, there is a regular flow in the number of those with a call to eliminate the shoddy method and dangerous machine. The job of the factory inspector calls for insight and understanding that comes of dedication to this cause. At the same time, and by the same token, a care for the effect of work on the lives of employees and their families is called for. A true goal of industry includes a commitment to the society that goes to make it up and a commitment that is not content with mediocre results.

Beyond the manufacturing or processing areas of industry lies the world of administration of accounts and of public relations. In these spheres the call to excellence cannot be too often stated. Practices such as bribery, price discrimination or collusion, dishonest advertising and overselling, unfairness in hiring and dismissals, and editing of accounts and reports, are known to flourish on a scale discreditable to business and in the long run damaging to its efficiency and ability to survive. What is to be done about them? Corruption is very insidious and the temptations to a generation that does not share the disciplines of religion are rampant. With such a weak moral framework on which to build, it is often very disheartening to set about a corrective attitude, but none the less it is important work. Are we as honest as we were as a nation? Does the City of London still proceed on the word given and not the written contract? Is it not because of the necessity of honesty in the face of corruption, of the reliability of a man's word in conveying contract or exchange that the British commercial scene has become as important as it is? The greatness of the British banks stems from the trust that was placed a hundred years ago in the hands of largely Quaker individuals of impeccable moral integrity. The origin of sterling as a reserve currency and of the City as the world centre of commerce goes back, in the last resort, to the puritanical integrity of the Protestant Reformation.

An important part of the answer lies simply and directly in the behaviour of top managers themselves. The behaviour of a man's superiors in the company is identified as the chief factor making for ethical or unethical practices. Business schools commonly find that top managers coming to their courses are concerned with the direction which they are to give their businesses by their own decisions, but middle managers are more concerned with how to adapt to decisions bearing down on them from above, and quite possibly carrying the business in a wrong direction. The first consideration must be to help existing and prospective top managers to develop a mature code of principles of their own. The vocation to maintain these standards has to be nurtured if it is not to be lost. Standards of truth in advertising are maintained by mutual dedication and vocation: standards in a company are not only maintained by a financial audit, but by a running moral or ethical audit within the company itself.

Vocation is severely tested in those determined to expose corruption, but today it is possible to trace the causes of corruption, dishonesty, and bad business all too often to the anonymity of many concerned. Sir Peter Runge writes:

> The ultimate in anonymity is the Civil Service and I have no doubt that we can all think of examples where this has led to questionable behaviour. And no doubt we all have our little hates. Mine concerns the tendency for bureaucracy to yield to importunity. There is the thick file theory which holds that you only get your way when the to and fro correspondence can no longer be threaded on to the lace of standard length. . . . That shafts are aimed at public services as well as at industry is a clear indication that it is not profit alone which breeds mistrust; there are other powerful factors amongst which the impersonality of large organizations rank very high.

That which is worked by the anonymous is rarely free from inertia and deception, whereas the declared policy, aims, and

M

promises of known individuals call out the best and establish a vocation to excellence. The individual, therefore, with a Christian vocation in commerce today finds he becomes a catalyst in the situation to which he is sent. He becomes the meeting-point of opposing views, and his presence may easily bring things to a crisis, or bring matters to a head. This may be an oversimplification, and this situation is what makes our thrillers so delightfully escapist. The man with a vocation will not find a simple situation of villains and heroes, but bring the moment of truth to many who would otherwise avoid it.

There stands an invitation to men with an industrial or commercial vocation to sit down and think through the ethical and moral results of their day-to-day decisions. In many ways it would be convenient if a 'case-book' on moral commercial practice was compiled, but such a compilation would inevitably lead to the errors of casuistry and the wrong in reducing Christian precepts to a moral code. Nevertheless examples of decisions involving moral conviction need working out and communicating. One can take the example of a company which produced a cake-mix of high quality. Few housewives could produce as good a cake from their own ingredients. However, its two-step preparation proved a stumbling block to that growing segment of the market that places a tremendous premium on ease, speed, and convenience. To meet the needs of these modern housewives a one-step cake-mix was developed which required just one minute from package to baking tin. Tests showed it did not equal the old-fashioned quality of regular cake-mix, yet for millions of housewives it was the preferred product. It was not economic to market both mixes. What should the company do? Or take the example of the company that markets a product which is sold primarily as a soft drink. However, it is in fact also an excellent alcoholic mixer—with gin or vodka. And not only good but also very cheap by comparison with other mixers on the market. The President of the company disapproves of alcoholic drink, so any reference in advertising and sales promotion to its properties as an alcoholic mixer are forbidden. This means that the company loses large sales as a result. Is the President of the company right or wrong to impose his own set of values on company policy in this way? Or, as an example of the kind one hears too often, take the head of a department in a company aged fifty-five. He is married with two sons at the university. His life is his work. He is now, however, rather too old for the job, and has lost the ability to inspire the people he has working for him. Several of the brightest young men in his department have left the company as a result of this situation. The Managing Director of the company decides to offer the man premature retirement. He knows this will be a great shock to the man, that financially he will be hard hit, and that being retired at fifty-five will produce enormous psychological problems for him. Yet he sees no alternative. Was the Managing Director right or wrong to take this decision?

Examples such as those mentioned do not lend themselves to treatment in the pulpit; they only respond to discussion, and begin to become resolved by the compilation of experience and the gathering together of a code-law affecting commercial morality. The need to extend and clarify this new realm of Christian awareness is a matter of some urgency. It is an integral part of Christian vocation in industry.

In any discussion, general or particular, concerning vocation the question must be asked whether this attitude to work is dependent on a religious motive? Does the atheist personnel officer with a strong sense of responsibility have a vocation? The answer to these questions lies in our use of the word religion. Inasmuch as dedication to the human race and its welfare without any commitment to God can be a real religion, then religion is an essential foundation for vocation. It is perhaps better to approach this issue by taking into account the historical circumstances and inherited attitudes that go to make up this 'religious' approach to work.

In these islands we are the heirs of a prophetic religion and a prophetic attitude to our society. It was the genius of the Jews in the first place that established an attitude of being called to be a people, the attitude of being a nation set apart for a purpose. This Hebrew interpretation of the role of the people of God, as exercising a mission to the rest of humanity, is an outlook from which the Christian cannot dissociate himself. Further, the Hebrew concept was taken up by Christ at a given time and place and enlarged so that the people with a mission were determined not by blood but by conviction. The new people of God were to be those who saw a new purpose in life, in death, in personal relationships, and in public morality. There was clearly in the mind of Christ not the slow conversion of the population, but the establishment of a committed minority. The parables spoken by he who completed the Jewish law and established a new law were frequently concerned with calling out not the masses but the few to act as a leaven in the lump. In all aspects of living the new people were enabled to see the new man, Jesus of Nazareth, establishing a new focal point for human destiny and a new pattern for human behaviour. In the writings of Teilhard de Chardin we are now being introduced not only to this concept of the Christian society being called out by God for a purpose, but also to the end product of the whole human race being incorporated in a new united humanity.

But leaving the long-term issues of the destiny of man and returning to the present situation of a secularized Europe, it is clear that vocation to serve belongs properly to both a religious conviction, in the broadest sense, and to a membership of a committed society called into being for a purpose. This society, the wider Church, has a distinctive morality, a human direction, and enjoys a promise of completion, all of which it would share with an ever-widening circle of human beings.

In addition to the sense of mission that the Christian community has inherited is the doctrine that the material world is good and not evil, and that the resources of the natural world are there to be respected and developed, as in partnership with a creator. This deep-down respect for the 'holiness' of matter enabled the Church in the medieval days to inaugurate scientific experiment, and still ensures that religion is not divorced from the matters of everyday existence. This Christian attitude to the world is perhaps best seen in contrast to the non-Christian attitude. The inherited religions of India and the East have been a denying ordinance on their followers: the material world has been that from which we must, at all costs, escape, and the force of this material world is the enemy for the Hindu, Buddhist, and other pantheistic religions alike. The absence of progress over hundreds of years in the underdeveloped countries in Africa and the East can be partly attributed to the common philosophy of denying the validity of material existence, even to the extent of hating it. Among such there has been little sense of the craftsman bringing stone, iron, or artistry into the service of the common good, and when education and affluence have begun to be felt there has been a comparatively small measure of duty in sharing the benefits. The contrast with the Christian philosophy of work and Christian acceptance of the material world is as radical as it is essential. It is true to say that the scientific and technological era that we are experiencing could have only been developed on the foundation of the Christian Western world.

Vocation therefore means partnership with God, partnership with humanity and with the unseen forces of love, joy, and peace which are known to be true. It means a humble subservience to the ever-developing knowledge of science, of the controls possible on humanity, and of the ever-increasing possibilities for our race that lie ahead. These are the spheres in which God is at work in addition to and more so than in the spheres of any religious society. Sometimes religious people feel a sense of regret when they discover this truth of the scientific age: they have a sense of betrayal, that God is not playing fair—in fact, God is instructing both the Church and wider humanity with new insights, new disciplines, and new structures which are as exciting as they are awe-inspiring.

Vocation certainly has a religious basis to a greater or a lesser extent, but it is in no sense confined to the Church or to the narrow limits of professionalism. It is the acceptance of greater truths than we can understand and of a better destiny for mankind than we dare hope. In obedience to this attitude is the ever-increasing opportunity for vocation in the industrial world.

14 | *A Case for Conscience*

by EDWARD HOLLOWAY

Edward Holloway is well known as a lecturer and writer on economic questions. He was co-founder of the Economic Reform Club, 1936; this organization now works in close co-operation with the Economic Research Council, of which he is the Hon. Secretary. He is also Director of the Commonwealth Industries Association.

Holloway stood for Parliament in the 1945 and 1950 elections. He played a significant part in the campaign which resulted in the appointment by H.M. Government of the Radcliffe Committee on credit and currency. In 1967 he sponsored the "Programme for National Recovery" signed by nineteen industrialists, economists, and writers. He is the author of *The Case for an Atlantic Free Trade Area*, published in 1967, and joint author of *Money: the Decisive Factor*, published in 1959.

There comes a moment in the lives of most successful men when they begin to query the true value of their contribution to society. For some this raises no problems; for others it does cause some considerable heart-searching which can sometimes lead to decisions being made which are both personally painful and financially unpleasant. Such a case, perhaps rather an extreme one, arose in pre-war days, where the contradictions between inner conviction and outward success led to such decisions being made. It requires a high degree of honesty and integrity to go against one's own personal interests, and it is certainly not always wise to go to the lengths of resignation as a means of forwarding one's objective. In this particular case, however, my own view is that it was the only course open to the individual concerned.

The father of all economists, Adam Smith, wrote: "It is not from the benevolence of the butcher, the brewer, or the baker, that we expect our dinner, but from their regard of their own interests. We address ourselves, not to their humanity, but to their self-love." That this is true of the majority of mankind few will deny. Yet there has always been a tiny minority of people, from all walks of life, who have deliberately put self-interest on one side for the sake of a cause in which they truly believe.

I have been fortunate in the years since 1930, when I first became interested in economic policy, and in particular monetary policy, to meet a number of such people. One outstanding character was certainly Vincent Cartwright Vickers. He was outstanding for two main reasons; firstly for his complete sincerity and honesty, and secondly for his disregard for personal aggrandizement. In his latter years his convictions drove him to take a course completely at variance with his own self-interest, yet he did this in such a disarming way that few were conscious of the very real sacrifices of wealth and health he was prepared to make for the cause in which he believed.

This was allied to a lively sense of humour, which enabled him to debunk so much of the hypocrisy which abounded in the 'good old days'. He was one of those fortunate people who inherited considerable wealth, in modern parlance 'a bloated capitalist'. Nine-tenths of his income came from investments, and in his day this gave him position and all those things to which most men aspire in a lifetime of hard work. He had all these things without effort, yet he dedicated himself to a cause which could only bring him opprobrium and even hostility from those with whom he was associated in the world of finance.

Vincent Vickers was born on January 16th, 1879, by which time the firm which bore his name had become a great power in the country. The demand for steel had grown rapidly in the nineteenth century, and the industry was expanding tremendously with all the demands being made in building railways, ships, bridges, and the vast developments of the first Industrial Revolution. The Sheffield firm of Vickers had prospered and grown enormously, and the name had become a household word the world over.

He went to Eton and then to Magdalen College, Oxford, and in course of time became a Director of Vickers, an appointment he held for twenty-two years. In 1910 he was invited to become a Director of the Bank of England. With characteristic modesty he always said of this appointment that it arose because he represented heavy industry, was about the right age, with the right kind of background, and at the same time he knew nothing at all about financial policy. This, he said, was an obvious reason for making him a Director of the Bank of England. He often told me of his experiences when he attended meetings of the Court of Directors. Montagu Norman was then Governor, and with other knowledgeable merchant bankers he formed a caucus who were able, with their intimate knowledge of the business of banking and finance, to ensure that their policies were accepted by the other members of the Court without very much trouble.

It was not for some years that Vincent Vickers began to query whether these policies were in the best interests of the country. He was very concerned with business affairs, he had many interests, and being a Director of the Bank of England carried considerable prestige, including being made a Deputy Lieutenant of the City of London! It was when he fell desperately ill and during the period when he was slowly recuperating that he began to use his critical faculties to re-examine the policies he had until then accepted without too much query.

This period of isolation from the pressing world of affairs provided an opportunity which he had so far lacked, and this enabled him to think out the effects on the country and its people of the rigid financial policies maintained by Montagu Norman. This period of analysis of economic and financial policies accepted by most politicians, industrialists, and others almost without question led him to the conclusion that the operation of this system had been a disaster. He resigned from the Bank of England in 1919, but it was not until the crucial decision to return to the gold standard in 1925 that his conscience drove him actively to oppose the policies of Montagu Norman and the Government of the day.

Of this decision he subsequently wrote:

Ever since that day in 1926, when not in arrogance but with humility I felt it my duty to explain to the Governor of the Bank of England that henceforth I was going to fight him and the gold standard and the Bank of England policy until I died, I have been an ardent money reformer, since when I have spent much time and money in advocating the necessity for a reform of the monetary system.

The Chancellor of the Exchequer responsible for carrying out the policy of the Bank of England was Winston Churchill. Perhaps the best tribute that could be paid to the correctness of the views of Vincent Vickers in his courageous head-on collision with the policies of Montagu Norman in 1926 was contained in the forthright condemnation by Winston Churchill of the decision to return to the gold standard. Speaking in the Budget debate in the House of Commons on April 21st, 1932, Churchill said:

When I was moved by many arguments and forces in 1925 to return to the gold standard I was assured by the highest experts, and our experts are men of great ability and of indisputable integrity and sincerity, that we were anchoring ourselves to reality and stability; and I accepted their advice. I take for myself and my colleagues of other days whatever degree of blame and burden there may be for having accepted their advice. But what has happened? We have had no reality, no stability. The price of gold has risen since then by more than 70 per cent. That is as if a 12-inch foot rule had suddenly been stretched to 19 or 20 inches, as if the pound avoirdupois had suddenly become 23 or 24 ounces instead of—how much is it? 16. Look at what this has meant to everybody who has been compelled to execute their contracts upon this irrationally enhanced scale. Look at the gross unfairness of such distortion to all producers of new wealth, and to all that labour and science enterprise can give us. Look at the enormously increased volume of commodities which have to be created in order to pay off the same mortgage debt or loan. Minor fluctuations might well be ignored, but I say quite seriously that this monetary convulsion has now reached a pitch where I am persuaded that the producers of new wealth will not tolerate indefinitely so hideous an oppression.
Are we really going to accept the position that the whole future development of science, our organization, our increasing co-operation and the fruitful era of peace and goodwill among men and nations; are all these developments to be arbitrarily barred by the price of gold? Is the progress of the human race in this age of almost terrifying expansion to be arbitrarily barred and regulated by fortuitous discoveries of gold mines here and there or by the extent to which we can persuade the existing cornerers and hoarders of gold to put their hoards again into the common stock? Are we to be

told that human civilization and society would have been impossible if gold had not happened to be an element in the composition of the globe?

These are absurdities; but they are becoming dangerous and deadly absurdities. They have only to be asserted long enough, they have only to be left ungrappled with long enough, to endanger that capitalist and credit system upon which the liberties and enjoyments and prosperity, in my belief, of the vast masses depend. I therefore point to this evil and to the search for the methods of remedying it as the first, the second and the third of all the problems which should command and rivet our thoughts.

There could be no clearer vindication of the views which V. C. V. placed before Montagu Norman in 1926, yet the main case which he put forward in the 1930's is still not accepted forty years later by the economic and financial pundits: that is, the need for an honest money system. As he put it, "We do not possess, and have never possessed, a true and honest measure of value." Although the orthodoxy of today is different from the orthodoxy of the 1930's, the monetary system still remains unsatisfactory, and the words V. C. V. wrote in 1939 are as true today as they were then: "I believe that the existing system is actively harmful to the State, creates poverty and unemployment, and is the root cause of war."

The last fifteen years of his life were spent, with other like-minded men and women, in a single-minded attempt to arouse his fellow-countrymen to the immense dangers inherent in an unsound monetary policy, and he based his case on his own very wide experience and knowledge gained from his years in industry and in the Bank of England. This meant resigning from many of his directorships, including that of the family firm of Vickers, Ltd., and it also meant that to many of his contemporaries he was labelled as a crank, with all that this implies in orthodox and respectable circles!

It is an interesting speculation to consider how very different would be the position of Britain today had his warning given in 1926 been heeded by the authorities. Looking back to the immense harm done to industry, to the well-being of millions of British people, to the unemployment with its accompanying degradation, to the malnutrition and poverty, to the destruction of good labour relations, it is surely obvious that had the suffering and misery brought about by the policy of deflation been avoided, the outlook and position of our country today could have been revolutionized.

There is no doubt that the trail of bitterness and frustration brought about by the existence of very nearly three million unemployed in 1930 could have been avoided, and today we are reaping the whirlwind in resistance to change, restrictive practices, go-slows, strikes, and many other manifestations of irrational behaviour. The memory of the traumatic experience of the thirties, when men, women, and children went hungry while we burned crops, poured milk down drains, and ruined many large and small enterprises, is largely responsible for much that goes wrong in human relations to this day. Recent reports from Common Market countries refer to the destruction of food in order to keep up prices, undoubtedly reinforcing such memories.

V. C. V.'s appeal was to common sense; he urged that the right course was to combine Christian principles with practical business abilities. To those who claimed that this was an 'impossible suggestion' he replied:

We do not ask you to unseat your Directors and put the bishops in their place, nor to introduce psalm-singing among your employees; but rather to carry on as you are now doing, with only one exception—an exception to which no industry will dare openly to object; even though it may seriously affect certain trades which, like the mistletoe, thrive upon others. We ask that you carry on your affairs as at present, except that you be honest—honest not only with others but with yourselves. It is not enough to be able to call a spade a spade; with others, as with yourselves, you must be able to put all the cards, and not only the spades, on the table, and to play the game throughout by the Christian principle of honesty.

Let us acknowledge the truth. Humanity is not suffering from unavoidable circumstances over which it has no control, but from the results of deliberate and dishonest actions of its own creation and invention. Fundamental laws, originally designed for the common welfare of the individuals of a community, have been broken—community laws which were never intended to permit the individual to grow fat upon the poverty of others, nor to permit him, in pursuit of his own personal profit, to base his standard of honesty upon his own flexible conscience, consoling himself with gratitude that he is within the law. Nevertheless, just as man has brought upon himself, or has permitted, this world tribulation, so can he play his part in undoing the harm that has been done.

Among his many gifts V. C. V. had a keen sense of humour, and the ability to tell a story which held his audience in a way that cannot be conveyed by the printed word. He was a born raconteur, and one of his favourite stories concerned the Bank of England. It was after he had resigned his Directorship and Britain had returned to a modified form of gold standard. Under these provisions holders of £2500 in notes were entitled to change them for an equivalent amount in gold specie. So one day he packed £2500 in notes in his brief-case and went along to the Bank of England to ask for a bar of gold. The clerk behind the counter was visibly worried by this unusual request; he had no knowledge of any such provision. After much consultation with higher authority he at last agreed that the transaction was in order, and the bar of gold was duly brought up from the vaults of the Bank. As he carefully wrapped this up in a piece of brown paper to hand to this unusual client, the clerk said, "Excuse me, Sir, but there has been much interest aroused in the Bank by your request. Could you tell me why you want a bar of gold?" To which V. C. V. replied, "I want to use it as a door-stop!"

Vincent Vickers died on November 3rd, 1939, after a long illness which sapped his physical strength. Yet he went on with his attempt to write and to put on record his convictions until the day he died. A few days before his death he wrote, "My keen desire to help up to the end has been the sole incentive which has enabled me to carry on perhaps a few weeks longer." Some twelve months after his death I was asked to go to an office in the City, and there I was handed a parcel containing a mass of papers which comprised all the notes, memoranda, and other writings which he had requested should be collected and handed to me after his death.

Much of this material was incomplete, and in his own hand-writing, which was not always a model of clarity. After struggling with this mass of material for some time, and realizing that in war-time conditions I had little hope of doing very much about it, I sent it on to his eldest daughter, Lady Cawdor. She wrote to me rather despairingly about it, but then suddenly she found it possible to put it all together in book form, and this was subsequently published by the Bodley Head under the title *Economic Tribulation*. It has been reprinted in the United States, Australia, and New Zealand, and has had a remarkable circulation all over the world.

Not all his views, written in the very differing circumstances of the 1930's, stand the test of time. Obviously much has happened to change the basic situation. The Bank of England has been nationalized. Instead of deflationary monetary policies, it is inflation which has been the problem in the years since the war, a condition which he would have regarded as equally dishonest. Nevertheless, there are still many points of value worthy of consideration even after the passage of so much time. He did not believe that any perfect cut-and-dried scheme was possible, but set out the main objectives to be achieved. These were:

1. State control and State issue of currency and credit through a central organization managed and controlled by the State.
2. Stabilization of the wholesale price level of commodities. That is to say, a fixed and constant internal purchasing power of money; so that a pound will buy tomorrow what it bought yesterday; an honest pound, not a fluctuating pound. And this can be done by so issuing and regulating the volume of available credit and currency that it shall at all times be adequate to permit of the purchasing power of the consumer being adequate with the volume of production; not by limiting the purchasing power but by firstly increasing purchasing power more in proportion to the productive capacity of industry.
3. Fixation of foreign exchanges by foreign exchange, equalization funds, and agreement with Empire countries and all other countries willing to fall into line; and once this was accomplished the removal or diminution of trade barriers which today protect the countries from the results of a bad monetary system.
4. Any additional supply of money should be issued as a clear asset to the State; so that money will be spent into existence, and not lent into existence.
5. The fluctuating quantity of gold lying in the vaults of the banking system should never be permitted to govern the volume of credit and currency needed by the country.

6. The elimination of slumps and booms; and more direct procedure for eliminating unnecessary poverty.
7. The abolition of the Debt System whereby all credit is created by the banks and hired out at interest to the country.

Other policies have prevailed in the years since V. C. V. died. No-one can claim that these have produced satisfactory results, either to Britain or in other countries. The inspiration of the last years of Vincent Vickers' life lives on, and there are many who are carrying on in the spirit of the opening words in his book *Economic Tribulation*:

"In so far as we are able, we must try to assist our fellow-men to understand. This we can do fearlessly, for that which is mistaken or false will carry no weight and will be lost and forgotten, whilst that which is true will prevail."

15 | Values and Enterprise as a Subject for Research

by REGINALD W. REVANS

Professor Revans took his B.Sc. degree at University College, London. He went to Cambridge University for his Ph.D., and was awarded a Commonwealth Fellowship which took him to the University of Michigan for three years. In 1935 he became Deputy Director of Education for Essex. In 1944 he was appointed Director of Education for the Mining Association and, upon nationalization, for the NCB.
In 1955 he became Professor of Industrial Administration, Manchester College of Science and Technology. In 1965 he became Senior Research Fellow for the European Association of Management Training Centres in Brussels.
He twice represented Great Britain at the Olympic Games.

The European Association of Management Training Centres has thirty-seven members in twelve different countries of Western Europe. It is a condition of membership that a centre either offers a management course to senior executives or engages in research in the field of general management. In the last few years the Association has been encouraging its individual members to work together, and across international frontiers, on research projects of common interest.

The titles of such common interests soon form a list so formidable that the resources of the thirty-seven centres are inadequate to tackle more than a few. Problems of international investment, of the effect of the Common Market, of the technological gap, and a hundred more: all these are of profound practical importance. Many of them are tackled already by individual centres, however, and the Association, concerned to apply its collective resources economically, does not wish to replicate what is being done already. But there are two questions of outstanding importance that are best approached collectively. The first affects the centres themselves; the second is thrown up by the enterprises for whom the centres try to provide. One question asks whether the courses run by the Association's members are of any value, and, if so, of what value? The other asks whether the businessmen of Europe observe an identifiable creed, specific to them, and, if so, what is that creed? In simple English, is there such a thing as a European business creed, and, if so, what is it?

This may strike an English industrialist as a strange question. It is undoubtedly an unusual one, because the Englishman, whether a businessman or not, is rarely given to the study of abstract general questions. There exists, for example, no word in English for translating the French word *finalité*; in so far as the word demands a phrase we should need to use some such clumsy construction as 'final objective to be defended on the Day of Judgment', or 'interpretation, in terms of the enterprise, of the set of values underlying all your behaviour', or, if so untheological a nation as the English can stand it, 'the inward spiritual grace of which life as a businessman is the outward visible sign'. It is even possible that English philosophy, from Locke, Berkeley, and Hume down to modern times, would deny that such a concept as *finalité* could be said to exist, since faith, in the final analysis, is an entirely personal concern. There is thus no reason to suppose that it can be common to a large number of persons, for as soon as it might be it is no longer personal and so no longer a faith. With these verbal conundrums, we are not, however, now concerned—though we might attack them with the fact that consultants talk freely of 'the medical conscience' of any given hospital. A responsible professional man, faced every day with a challenge to his beliefs, very soon recognizes great differences between the ways in which these might find expression in different communities; there is clearly some collective value system likely to affect his behaviour, and, whether this is called the *esprit de corps*, the atmosphere, or the morale of the organization does not, for our purpose, affect the issue; whatever we choose to call the observable quality of the professional conduct, it can be interpreted as the expression of a conscience, a creed, an ethic, a code of beliefs or, quite simply, of a system of final values.

Penultimate Values or Institutional Beliefs

The directors of Firm X, let us suppose, discuss practical affairs—suggesting decisions D_1, D_2, D_3 . . . and so forth. D_1 might be about a possible take-over bid; D_2 about a change in bank rate; D_3 about a proposal to launch a new product. It is clear that the discussions will involve not only the final value systems of the group of directors, but also their appreciation of what the enterprise—as distinct from other enterprises—is trying to do, or ought to be doing, or can do, or finds worth while doing. Thus, any general value system respected by the managers of any given culture is the local value system of the particular enterprise. It is this local value system, or at least the extent to which it is expressed, that gives the firm its reputation, high or low, among other firms, in the district from which it draws its labour and in the market through which it sells its products. It is possible to study this local value system in a perfectly objective way, as the following example shows.

Supposing that the discussions leading into decisions D_1, D_2, D_3, etc. . . . are taken down on a tape-recorder and analysed by content. What type of comments do the directors pass? How do they relate specific aspects of the matter under discussion, such as the proposed new product, to existing activities, such as their present salesmen-customer relations, or their long-established distribution channels, built up over many years, of friendly contact with certain retail stores? . . . There are obviously a very large number of implications, not specifically set out in the design and price of the new product but most important in their bearing upon the commercial policies of the enterprise. How far, in any kind of discussion, not only about D_3, the decision, say, on the new product, do the directors analyse, whether deliberately or not, the relation between the firm and the outlet channels? How important do they regard their reputation, not only with the ultimate consumer, but with the retailer? In some industries this may be a matter not only of goodwill but also of hard economics, involving difficult decisions about stocking policy, credit terms, advertising strategy, and so forth. Is it possible, by being sufficiently attentive to the tape-recordings, to recognize that, behind all the discussions, the directors constantly imply a concern for their good standing with their retailers?

Quite evidently, a search of the discussions, paying as much

attention to the asides and to the jokes as to the more structured parts of the agenda, will show that, for any particular
firm, there are several main themes running through all aspects
of major policy. These themes are a mixture of what the
directors, as the human beings they happen to be, think are
ultimately worth while and what are the particular or local
goals for which their enterprise should be striving. If a search
is actually made of a set of discussions in a particular boardroom
it will be found that topics such as the following needs
constantly emerge:

(*a*) to follow those lines of action that suggest future
growth;

(*b*) to ensure some minimum return on invested capital;

(*c*) to maintain a favourable public image;

(*d*) to keep good relations with employees;

(*e*) to be seen as technological leaders in the market;

(*f*) to retain the selection and promotion of future managers within the hands of the present directors;

(*g*) to improve the rewards and conditions of service of the
present directors.

It may then be asked whether such identification of the basic
needs of the enterprise, as they are seen by those in charge of it,
can be of any use, either to the research worker looking for
truth *sub specie aeternitatis* or to the policy-making board members, curious to know something of their mutual interactions
and common motivations.

The particular list of themes that can be described in the
deliberations of particular companies will be, to some extent,
singular to the company itself; each list will, however, contain
items proper to all the firms in a given industry. For example,
in the electronics industry a large number of firms will assume
the need to strive for technological leadership in the market.
In industry, in general, many firms will wish to grow, and all
will desire some minimum return upon invested capital. Many
other firms will have quite different items upon their hidden
agenda, such as, for example, wishing to become a public
company or marshalling their resources to repel a take-over

bid. However this may be, in the deliberations of any given board it is possible to identify a list of eight or nine leading themes. Suppose now that a pack of eight or nine cards is printed, each with the title of one of the identified themes. As many packs of these cards are printed as there are directors of the enterprise; these directors are then offered each a pack of cards arranged in completely random order and the directors are invited, *without discussing the exercise with each other*, to put the eight or nine cards in what they consider to be their order of importance. The exercise is conducted anonymously so that whoever assembles the packs of cards does not know which has been ranked by whom. An array is then drawn up on a sheet of paper showing how each of the ten, fifteen, twenty, twenty-five or whatever number it may be of directors has ranked the eight or nine themes. An inspection of this array will at once reveal how far there is any common view among the directors of the enterprise as to what are their underlying value systems. The results are always of great interest. All may well agree that value X is respected by each of them, but some may place value X first, others may place it at the bottom. On the contrary, the man who places X at the top may place Y at the bottom and vice versa. There is a branch of statistical analysis which enables us to look at the array and to measure the extent to which all directors place the same relative importance upon the same values. This is thus a measure of the concordance or harmony among the group, and when this experiment is done it can be shown that there are immense differences between boards of directors in their relative degrees of harmony or of disagreement. It may well be that the best boards are those in which there is not too much agreement and not too little; where everybody agrees, serious issues are not seriously discussed, and where the relative value systems are a complete jumble there can only be discord that is actually destructive. If every individual director remembers the order in which he ranked his own set of cards and later is able to compare it with the overall array he may be able to draw some instructive conclusions; it is, of course, cardinal that the chairman of the board should be aware of the divergences that exist, even although, if the experiment is to be of any use, he cannot know which of his colleagues returned which particular rank order of values.

European Research Group on Management

Studies of this kind—that is, involving only the introspection of managers—can obviously be conducted across international frontiers. The European Research Group on Management, popularly known as ERGOM, has a set of standard exercises, originally designed by Professor Bernard M. Bass of the University of Pittsburgh, that have been translated into most European languages and subjected to the most rigorous comparisons. One particular set of exercises tempts managers not only to say what are their own life goals, but to assess how far their colleagues who know them agree with the manager's own evaluation. For example, if a manager within a group who know each other well says that his first life goal is self-realization, while his colleagues are unanimous that his first objective is physical comfort or prestige, then it is clear that either the manager is deceiving himself or that he holds an unusual view of the nature of self-realization. This, to sophisticated company directors, may seem an artless pastime; a man consumed with a desire for wealth and power is hardly likely to say so, and will rather try to give the impression of wishing to use his gifts for the benefit of humanity as a whole. But the exercises have many internal checks for consistency, and, moreover, the self-judgment of the individual has to be measured against the verdict of his colleagues. Nor is this all. The results of many thousand such trials are fed into a computer, and it is possible to write down the priorities in different countries and in different industries. These experiments are only just beginning, but it is nevertheless already clear that, for example, among salesmen of highly complex products such as computers the first desire is to be seen as an adviser on the customer's problem rather than as a collector of substantial commission, whereas the man's boss, the sales director, judges the salesman to rate his commission above his advice. There are also marked differences between nations. This confirms the work of Professor Mason Haire of MIT, whose book *Managerial Thinking* has shown vast differences between different continents.

The value of such work is not so much perhaps the statistical results that emerge from it, as the way in which these attempts to define preferences focus attention upon whatever it may be that managers hold to be worthwhile.

Theory and Practice

These approaches are very new and may be a little ingenuous. They have necessarily needed to await the growth of research in the human sciences and a better understanding of statistics. They remain at the level of marks on paper, and one of the extraordinary qualities of human beings is that they may be highly consistent in their purely intellectual responses but yet behave in a manner quite inconsistent with their expressed beliefs. The learned author of a three-volume work upon philosophy or even ethics may nevertheless fly into a rage if any of his beliefs are questioned by a colleague. It is well known that what men say and what the same men do—and what in their innermost hearts they may believe—are not seldom opposed. Thus, true research into the value systems of managers demands not only that researches of the type so far described should enable us to know what men say they believe and measure the inconsistencies with which they say it; it should also enable us to compare what they say with what they do and with how other people interpret why they are doing it.

For example, Napoleon, when placing one or other of his brothers upon the throne of some dispossessed monarch, would invariably advise him to make plenty of speeches about liberty, on the one hand, but to ensure that nobody secured any liberty, on the other. But had there been social scientists at the time, some would have imagined that Napoleon, in overthrowing the royal tyrants, was granting liberty, while others, observing Napoleon only to exchange one despotism for another, would deny that he was granting liberty to anybody. Hence we need to know, not only what the man himself professes, and what he actually does, but how others interpret both his speeches and his actions. Freedom has had a multitude of interpretations, and this is no place to comment on what they might have meant. Nevertheless, the field of study is clearly before us, and the management schools of Europe, in drawing up their research policies in 1967, placed the study of managerial value systems at the top of their list; more management schools across Europe expressed an interest in working with each other on the question "Is there such a thing as a European business creed? If so, what is it?" than upon any other single topic. One school in the Netherlands which has been studying this problem for nearly two years joined the European Association of Management Training

Centres solely to widen its contacts in this area of research. The studies consist in reading the speeches of leading industrialists, whether made on purely general occasions like public functions or celebrations, on regular occasions, such as the presentation of annual reports, or on special occasions, such as crises in industrial relations, the opening of new factories, the launching of new products, or the securing of exceptional contracts. It is possible to make a content analysis of these remarks and to identify, as in the experiments described above, the main values assumed by the speaker. Several lines of inquiry are then opened up. How far, for example, would other members of the management recognize these same values? Supposing, for instance, a small number of colleagues within the same firm or of its middle management or drawn from among the supervisors were interviewed, using the speech of the man at the very top as the framework for the interview, how far would what he said be reflected throughout his management team? What kind of interpretation would his competitors put upon his remarks—after, of course, making due allowance for the fact that they were competitors? What about the rank and file? We are said to be a democratic nation, and the majority is always supposed to be right. Without being so simple-minded as to believe this proposition to be true, it can nevertheless be instructive to know how the majority interpret the words of their leader. How, too, is the enterprise judged to act when it faces a crisis? Does its observed behaviour bear any relation to its declared policies? What happens to the faith when it is cast into the crucible?

There are many observers of what the firm may say and what it may do other than its own management and its own trade unionists. We live in an age of publicity, and there are Press commentators of many kinds, from the popular dailies to the highly informed economic and political analysts of international repute. A good research project will not only compare the declarations of the enterprise with its actual performance; it will ask what the commentators say they see. It may then interview the commentators and find in their hearts they believe something quite different from what appears in their avidly consumed daily columns. It would, for example, be to insult the writers of Britain's most popular journals to suggest that, as human beings, they actually believe what they write. The researches of the school in the Netherlands show that it is possible to produce order in this tangle of expressed opinion, overt behaviour, public comment, true belief, etc. But then who is to check upon the structure built into all this by one particular school? Holland is a nation with a particular religious history, and this may colour the perception of its professors. What is therefore needed is that a number of schools, drawing their ideas from different ethical, economic, and religious backgrounds, should co-operate with each other in making these assessments. When the management schools of different European countries, especially if they can co-operate with the schools of America and Eastern Europe, are allowed to argue with each other as to the frame of co-ordinates needed for describing what managers think they believe in, we may secure some interesting results. It is not that we may hit upon some final creed, placing personal, social, and economic values in some objectively true order of importance, but it is quite realistic to suggest that a careful and structured study across international frontiers of what men say they believe, how they can be observed to act, and how they are judged by their fellows, may throw a great deal of light upon the contradictions of business policy.

It is clear that no such research can be done unless those who live by industry, whether manager or worker, will permit it to be done. It is also highly likely that this permission will not be granted unless those trying to do the research have some realistic hypotheses that they would like to test. Industry has embarrassments enough already without being asked to give up its valuable time to idle and curious inquisitors. Foremost among these hypotheses would, in my view, be one about the nature of profit. Much of the controversy which seems to bedevil industry in Europe and in America depends, not so much upon a value system that either accepts or rejects the notion of profit, as upon a sheer inability to discriminate between profitability and profit itself. An enterprise that is unprofitable —that is, which in its total context consumes more than it produces—is an enterprise which seems to challenge a fundamental notion in any value system. If man's first need is to secure maximum control over his environment he should, in any economic system, be giving attention to activities that are a pure waste of time and effort, and such activities one may describe as unprofitable. On the other hand, the enterprise that produces more than it consumes, that uses the time and talents of men to produce more than that with which they started, is a profitable enterprise, and I know of no value system which denies its goodness. The question, however, as to how the yield of this profitable enterprise is then to be shared among those responsible for making it profitable—and any others who might stand to benefit—is an entirely different one, but perfectly consistent with the value system that accepts profitability as the aim of all human endeavour. It is because in the past insufficient thought has been given to our basic value systems that this confusion, between the action being worth while and the division of the benefits of its worth-whileness, has crept into the counsels of mankind. Much of the strife and misunderstanding that bedevils industry is not over the nature of profitability but over the division of its consequences. We all know that these lofty arguments reduce to the homely truth that one cannot divide a cake which is not there. This simple proverb, however, comes a little too late on the scene, and we need to examine throughout all the processes of our economic and technological bakehouse the contradictions between what men say and what men do, for it is these that in the end determine whether or not any cake at all will emerge.

16 | Business and Ethics

by SIMON WEBLEY

Simon Webley was born in Bristol and educated at Blundell's and Trinity College, Dublin, where he read economics and political science. For five years he worked with the Reed Paper Group in their economic research unit. Then as a consultant, lecturer, and writer on economic and management subjects. He was Deputy Director of the Industrial Educational and Research Foundation, and is now Research Director of the British North American Committee.

Whether one agrees or not with the contention of a distinguished American Chief Justice that "in civilized life Law floats in a sea of Ethics", it is a fact that the practices and behaviour of industrialists and their companies are considered by many to be less ethical than those of, say, the professions. Indeed, industry's reputation when it comes to ethical matters is generally considered to be sub-standard.

There are probably two main causes for this. The first is inherent in the very nature of business. If profitability is the principal aim and object of an organization, then in the mind of the man in the street every action and decision is by definition aimed at achieving this, whatever the means. This attitude is extremely prevalent and adversely affects many aspects of industrial life: for instance, it directly influences a firm's ability to recruit first-class people, and at the same time it hinders businessmen's ability to speak clearly on issues which face society for fear of ridicule. A sort of corporate inferiority complex appears to produce an almost apologetic attitude. Only when the objectives of companies are openly attacked will some of the more clear-minded top executives speak out in defence of, for instance, making profits. Ethical considerations, however, play a significant part in making profits in the majority of public and private companies. Directors readily admit that if the organization is to survive and grow as well as maximize their return on capital employed, they must take

account factors other than those that are strictly
~~~ercial.

~~~sides the inherent nature of business, the other cause of
the tarnished reputation of industrialists when it comes to
ethical issues is the disproportionate amount of publicity
which is focused on the revelations of sharp practice or
misconduct when they do occur.

It is unfortunate that the misdemeanours of the few seem
to affect adversely the standing of the whole. This multiplier
effect does not affect the professions to nearly the same extent.
When, for instance, a solicitor or a doctor is accused of some
unethical practice the disciplinary committee of the relevant
profession establish the facts and, if the accused is found
guilty, apply whatever sanctions are appropriate. The effect
on the general public is to restore confidence in the profession
generally. Perhaps it is because there is no such disciplinary
mechanism in business (apart from the law of the land) that
sections of the public have such a low regard for business when
it comes to ethical matters.

Attempts have been and are being made to establish management as a profession—Institutes of Management exist in a
number of countries, and though admissions and registrations
vary, nearly all are by experience rather than examination.
Furthermore, where disciplinary committees have been established none have been given any real power. Part of the difficulty
has been to establish and codify the knowledge and skill
required in a manager. Even where this has been achieved the
problem of setting up standards of performance which can be
tested and the establishment of a code of ethical behaviour
which is generally accepted have up to now proved insuperable
problems. Within management a number of functional professionals usually practise—e.g., engineers and accountants—
but however high the standard of ethics in their profession, it
does not follow that the same standards are adhered to when
it comes to their role as managers. In the United Kingdom
today there is still no recognized profession of management.
However, with the upsurge of education and training of
management, the complex problem of defining standards of
management practice may be nearer solution. Perhaps one of
the clearest discussions of this problem was by the American
Paul Donham,[1] in an article "Is Management a Profession?"

He concludes that business cannot be a profession because in the course of achieving its object there will arise circumstances that are unacceptable within a professional code of behaviour. Others have taken a different view. The Institute of Industrial Administration Professional Standards Committee in 1951 stated that the question of professional standards for a body concerned with general management was not substantially different from that of the well-established professions—even when this meant the acceptance of a code of ethics guaranteeing the public trustworthiness and competence. Sir Hugh Beaver in 1952, addressing the British Institute of Management, stated that the professional side of management needed to be developed, and study was needed on how best to achieve this. He pointed out that the most difficult research lay in the area of the philosophy of management, the basic underlying qualities which made up such a philosophy, and the ultimate aims of management.

In an age where there is an increasing awareness of the need of business for competent management and where education is being provided to make it possible for a growing number to receive comprehensive training in management subjects, there is also a paramount need for standards. This would enable those who hire management, those who work with managers, and those who are outside industry to have a yardstick to which to refer. Managers who purposely flout even the minimum standards of community behaviour invite the attention of legislators, and as a result managers who are both reputable and competent find their activities are often the subject of minute investigation and, in due course, very often find themselves constricted by law.

Whether or not it is possible for business in general or management in particular to formulate a code of ethics which is both acceptable and enforceable, it is important to bring to the attention of all those responsible for decisions in business, whether in the boardroom or at the Union meeting, the need for moral standards.

Business and commerce provide employment and hence influence the lives of the majority of men and women of the industrialized countries. Scientific and technological advances are leading to larger organizations and international competition. The western world is moving towards a few very large international corporations which together will control a considerable proportion of the resources of many nations. Inevitably the question is being asked regarding the responsibility of these companies to the various nations in which they operate and to the individuals who are employed by them. Decisions made by a very small number of people affect the personal lives of millions. Society is questioning whether this is right or acceptable. Industrialists in responsible positions faced with such questions must not only be competent but coherent in their answers.

The basic dilemma for the leader in business (whether on the board or in the union) is the reconciliation of competing ends. For example, there is a measure of conflict in most companies between the rightful requirements of the owners (shareholders), the customers, the employees, and the community.

These claims are never easy to reconcile, and an increasing number of board members are asking for guidance about decisions which have an ethical or moral content. In the United States some detailed surveys have taken place on current practice in business regarding ethical standards and social responsibilities. In an interesting book with the title *Social Responsibilities of Businessmen*[2] Howard Bowen states:

> The first and most essential condition, if social responsibility is to become a more effective force, is that businessmen must acquire a strengthened sense of vocation. They must accept the social implications of their calling. They must recognize that ultimately business exists not for profits, for power, or for personal aggrandizement, but to serve society.

This may be an oversimplification of the problem, but it does raise the issue of how ethical businessmen are. Unfortunately in the United Kingdom no objective study, as far as I can trace, has been made of this. However, in America Raymond Baumhart[3], a Jesuit priest, while at the Harvard Business School undertook a major survey on behalf of the *Harvard Business Review* on this subject. Its findings are not irrelevant to the United Kingdom scene. Four out of five executives who ventured an opinion stated that there were practices in their companies which, though generally accepted, were none the less unethical. Another survey of "On the Job Ethics"[4] shows that similar views were expressed by employees about their practices.

The major areas where ethical standards are suspect in industry are:

(*a*) The use of bribery of one sort and another to obtain preferential treatment.

(*b*) Collusions on pricing and market-sharing, although forbidden by law.

(*c*) Misleading promotional material.

(*d*) The treatment of employees, especially older ones.

(*e*) Falsification of expenses and other matters involving money.

(*f*) Pressure from above leading to practices which may compromise personal integrity.

Many more examples could be given, and, indeed, whole books written on this subject. At the same time a similar list of examples of honesty and high ethical standards in industry could be compiled. Merely to enumerate symptoms of disease or health is not a particularly useful exercise. What is necessary is to examine the causes which give rise to malpractice.

Industry, and its handmaid commerce, exist primarily to provide goods and services to satisfy human needs. The incentive to organize the various elements which make up a business —at any rate, in the democracies—is the profit that can be made from such operations. This is not only the entrepreneur's reward for risk-taking, but is also a measure of his efficiency and how far he is successful in satisfying the requirements of his customers.

It follows that quality, price, marketing practice, and the relationship with employees and customers all have a significant effect on whether the business thrives or deteriorates. The enterprise system as opposed to the planned system uses the customer and the market-place. Of course, the system is open to abuse; however, it is preferred by the majority because of its underlying assumptions regarding freedom of choice which is so limited under a planned system. Thus businessmen are encouraged to pursue efficiency, cost minimization, and profit targets, and their responsibilities lie here. If the business executive undertakes extramural responsibilities—local government, a charitable committee—this is agreeable. But he will be judged not on his good works but on his ability to meet targets and produce profit. It is precisely in this area that so much misunderstanding arises. In the United Kingdom the social function of profit is understood only by a minority. So often profit is equated with self-interest, and the misunderstanding places the business enterprise in a vulnerable moral position. As a result, when industry puts forward sensible and well-thought-out suggestions for changes in the social structure its suggestions are looked on with considerable suspicion and apprehension by other parts of the community. It was to try and correct this situation that the idea of the Press and Public Relations Officer appeared. His task was to present the company or industry in the best possible light and to explain carefully its policy to all inquirers. His role is not to hide the truth. Reputable P.R. men refuse positions where their task is to gloss over dubious and unethical practices.

There is now some evidence that industrialists generally are becoming more sensitive to ethical values. In the United Kingdom there have recently been cases of alleged excess profits by some firms on Government contracts, and a City code of takeovers and mergers has been drawn up, based on the principle of self-discipline. In the United States the growing literature and discussion of ethics and morals in business is now having some effect on practice. Professor Michael Fogarty in *Wider Business Objectives—American Thinking and Experience*[5] elaborates on where the pressures to think about objectives are coming from. Where business has failed to understand the necessity of adapting its policies to what can be described as public requirements nothing but difficulty has resulted. The more industry has been constrained by law to put its house in order, the lower has been the incentive to innovate and be enterprising. The difference between regulation and control is narrow but crucial. Regulations in matters of, say, safety, have brought considerable benefit to both industry and society. But controls, where they have been applied, have in the main been disruptive. Unfortunately industry in general has been slow to regulate its own behaviour. Lip-service is paid to the competitive system as being beneficial to society as a whole, and yet monopoly and restrictive trade practice legislation is often bitterly opposed. At the other end of the scale union reforms are also resisted passionately by many. The defence of the United

States General Electric Company executives who were given prison sentences for breaking the U.S. Anti-trust laws appears at first sight to be morally sound. The reasons were:

1. A desire to keep members employed during a time of poor business.
2. A desire to make sure their company had enough money to engage in research that would help public and private utilities, and
3. A desire to protect their companies from sharp competitive practices.

Yet in essence these men were rejecting the idea of competition which the State required.

In this situation individual moral standards and the social ethic (given the force of law) met head on.

As Victor Obenhause has pointed out in *Ethics for an Industrial Age*[6], generally businessmen change their practice only under pressure. Society is slow to organize itself to bring such pressure, but once it has set up organizations like the Consumers' Council, with its insatiable hunger for sponsors of Private Members Bills, it can, through such pressure groups, become a powerful irritant to business. The existence of the Consumers' Council certainly acts as a check on the temptation, for instance, to make false claims in advertising and to distribute in misleading containers. Such bodies as the Advertising Standards Authority, sponsored by the Advertising Association and the British Code of Advertising Practice, subscribed to by all the leading organizations in the field, are good examples of a profession putting its house in order.

The fact that pressure appears to be the motivating force rather than conscience is significant. It is perhaps a sign of the failure of religious ethics as such to come to grips with the moral dilemmas of the businessman that has in turn brought the charge of irrelevance to organized religion in industrial societies. However, current failure does not mean that, for instance, the Christian Gospel has no implications for businessmen. Indeed, there are a growing number of examples of businessmen who have discovered the relevance of the Christian message for themselves and have then applied its principles to business. There is nothing new in this. The Quaker businessman of the nineteenth century showed how practical a high moral and ethical sense was when it came to treatment of employees and customers. When the individual Christian brings his beliefs to bear on business decisions a change of ethical standards very quickly takes place.

Some businessmen have advocated the drawing up of formal codes of ethical practice for each company. Where such codes exist they constitute the lowest common denominator and, of course, must rely on voluntary acceptance. This is their weakness. There is, as far as can be traced, no business school in the United Kingdom that has any place for discussion of business ethics in its formal syllabus. Where it is discussed it is incidental. American experience leads to the conclusion that management training which merely teaches decision-making and its techniques in a vacuum will produce a breed of managers who are technically sound but socially unacceptable, and as such may well lead businessmen into further conflict with society.

Information is practically unobtainable regarding what guidance an executive draws upon when faced with an ethical decision. Observation shows that in the majority of cases the problem is passed upwards. It has been said that if you want to act ethically find an ethical boss. If this is true, then a heavy responsibility rests on leaders in business to set high standards. Perhaps some form of training for chief executives would be welcome on this subject. Moral theology, if it links man's relationship with his creator to man's relationship with his neighbours, should have much to contribute on these matters; it should provide the answer to those who are concerned with final responsibilities and ultimate loyalties. It is legitimate to ask in conclusion if corporate ethics can exist for the group, be it a business or any other social grouping, any more than for the individuals who make up the group? Those who claim that a corporate ethic can be developed point to the fact that, in many groupings in society, tradition and standards go hand in hand. The City Livery companies are an example. But industry is a much more loosely knit type of organization; the turnover of personnel is increasing; traditions are suspect. In these circumstances a corporate ethic as such is unlikely to be sustained for any long period. If this is true, then the matter becomes one for the individual.

1 Paul Donham, "Is Management A Profession?" (*Harvard Business Review*, September–October 1962).

2 Howard R. Bowen, *Social Responsibilities of the Businessman* (New York, Harper and Row, 1953).

3 "How Ethical are Businessmen?" (*Harvard Business Review*, July–August 1961), and Raymond Baumhart, *Ethics in Business* (New York, Holt, Rinehart, and Winston, 1969).

4 William H. Cohen Jr, in "On the Job Ethics" (Department of Church and Economic Life, National Council of Churches of Christ in the U.S.A., 1963).

5 Professor Michael Fogarty, *Wider Business Objectives—American Thinking and Experience* (Political and Economic Planning, May 1966).

6 Victor Obenhause, *Ethics for an Industrial Age* (London, John Wiley and Sons, Ltd, 1967).

o

17 | The Social Setting for

Modern Personnel Management

by SOLOMON BARKIN

Solomon Barkin was born in New York City in 1907. He was educated at the College of the City of New York and Columbia, and was Wertheim Fellow in Industrial Relations at Harvard University. After a period as Instructor at the College of the City of New York he was appointed to the New York State Commission on Old Age Security. In 1933 he became Assistant Director, Labour Advisory Board, N.R.A., and in 1935 Assistant Director, Labour Studies Section, Labour Advisory Board, N.R.A., and a year later Chief of the Labour Section, Division of Industrial Economics, U.S. Department of Commerce. From 1937 to 1963 he was Director of Research, Textile Workers Union of America. During the years 1959–62 he was Adjunct Professor of Industrial Relations, Columbia University Graduate School of Business. He was Visiting Professor of Economics, Graduate School, New School of Social Research, New York, 1961–62 and in 1963 became Deputy to Director and Head of Social Affairs Division, Manpower, and Social Affairs Directorate, O.E.C.D. His books include *Old Age Security; The Older Workers in Industry; Sub-Standard Conditions of Living;* and *The Decline of the Labour Movement and what can be done about it.*
Professor Barkin is married, with three children.

Man is affected by changes in his environment, but he is also constantly altering its nature and its influence upon him. While he cannot escape it he can nevertheless broaden his understanding of it and improve physical and social institutions and policies. Research of outer space has already brought many significant by-products, better communications, more precise knowledge about weather, and thousands of new instruments and technical innovations which have changed the material basis of our life. Innovations in our economy are producing comparable changes in the way it operates.

However much the physical, technical, and economic

210

environments have been altered—and these changes have conditioned our behaviour—it is man's concept of his purpose and goals which finally determines his future. It decides the direction of his search for inventions and, of course, sets the use to which resources are placed. Man's concept of his own destiny is reflected in the priorities assigned to immediate and long-term needs, to material advances and personal development.

We should therefore define the cultural and ideological setting and forces at work just as the material and economic ones. It is particularly necessary to operate successfully the field of personnel and industrial relations. These policies and practices should represent the adaptation of the values of our society to the employment of men in our economy.

The New Social Goals

The modern era bringing new aspirations was ushered in during the war. The social idealism of the pre-war years was channelled into new hopes which gave meaning to the war-time sacrifices. Man went into battle with the promise of new vistas. These aspirations were converted into commitments towards mankind to make the post-war world 'the age of the common man'. President Roosevelt and Prime Minister Churchill pronounced new guarantees, the four freedoms. From these undertakings sprang the decision to create a society of full employment adopted at the Philadelphia International Labor Conference of 1944.

Protection was to be provided not only for the productive members of society but also for those being nurtured for adulthood, those who had suffered incapacity, and the aged. The new 'Welfare State' promised to provide services and minimum guarantees of livelihood for people from the cradle to the grave. The last twenty years have witnessed a constant stream of efforts to give concrete meaning to the commitment. Social-security funds and social services have been extended. But we are still far from realizing the goal. It remains an enduring objective to which societies are dedicated and the yardstick by which Governments and employers are tested. Shortcomings in achievement and lapses in efforts are recurrently the subject of protest to advance the realization of this goal.

As the initial stage of European reconstruction drew to a close the vision of continued economic growth fired the imagination of men. It gave a new meaning to the faith in progress born in the last century. Specific tests of achievements were added. Full employment was to be accompanied by economic growth and rising living standards. Inevitably these obligations had to be reconciled with those of reasonable price stability, for it was generally recognized that runaway inflation could bring disaster. Most people were responsive to working in a setting which recognized this essential condition.

The assurance of man's right to participate in determining his own destiny became a third axiom in economic and social development. Political democracy has been the battle-cry of the nineteenth and twentieth centuries. It has been much abused, distorted, and debased, but the desire for it has never been destroyed. However capricious and unfruitful the experience may have been, demand for it has never been suppressed for long. The ordinary citizen recurrently gives his blood in this cause.

In the last century there was a general cry for 'industrial democracy', and this idea had an equally chequered development. Its application has taken diverse forms, but these have nevertheless been tangible. They have progressed from varied types of collective bargaining to claims for information, consultation, and, finally, participation in management. Many experiments and proposals have been tried, and more ideas remain to be tested. The concept still has to be refined, given specific meaning, and tried for enduring viability. But the hope remains deeply rooted in the minds of men.

Among the various social goals which have taken on new life in this post-war era there is a new one which builds on those already embedded in our collective heritage. It calls for real equality of opportunity. It is based on the belief that the individual desires to participate as an equal and share in the common labours of the community and his peers. The emphasis is on helping the individual to attain equality of opportunity. Protection is passive; intended for those who now or in the future are unable to rise to a position of equality. Societies committed to expansion must afford people the opportunity to build up their competences and participate fully in the community. The community is reaching out to these marginal persons to give them the opportunity to become equal members of the nation. In truth the 'Opportunity Age' is becoming a complement to the 'Welfare State'. It looks to the dwindling of the dependent adult groups in the nation.

The New Labour Market

The new social goals have not remained vague statements of purpose. They have been implemented in varying degrees and have affected the actual policies and activities of men. They are transforming our economies and social systems. Other forces are also shaping the new era. They have brought changes in the labour market, and are therefore particularly pertinent to a discussion of personnel and industrial-relations philosophies and practices.

The most outstanding phenomenon is no doubt the existence of full employment. Seldom before in the history of Western nations has a free labour market offered so widely such abundant opportunities for man to engage in productive employment. The existing labour resources have been absorbed and in most industrial European countries secondary working groups have been sifted for eligible persons. Those who have not been engaged in the first wave of recruitment have been enlisted later. Groups seldom considered as qualified have also been added as managements have learned to redesign jobs, workplaces, working conditions, demands and schedules. Where these domestic sources of labour proved inadequate managements turned to foreign workers. First they recruited those available in neighbouring countries. When they found their needs continuing to grow they extended their recruitment to more distant areas. Finally, the total rose to more than five millions. But the scarcities in labour supply persisted. Where the numbers of unskilled or untrained workers were sufficient, inadequacies showed up among the middle and professional grades. New occupations drew people away from the older ones. Demand for labour became the foremost problem in management; labour scarcity began to rank alongside shortages of other factors of production and now demanded greater sophistication in the management of enterprises and economies.

Economic expansion meant not only new construction and employments, but also the conversion or even the contraction of the old. The claims of the newer industries began relatively to outdistance older ones. Established ways of employment and job preparation no longer sufficed. Jobs were by nature different and demanded new competences and qualities. Old skills died out. What was even more significant was the new ratios of different types of jobs. Unskilled employments have been yielding to the machine operators and tenders and to assembly-line tenders. The content of skilled work has become more theoretical. White-collar work is being converted into machine-operation; technicians and professionals are multiplying and gaining a new ascendancy. A new amalgam of jobs has begun to appear; the 'white-coverall worker', a combination of technician and white-collar employee whose job is in the production processes which now include many clerical-type operations. Management itself is being converted into a profession. Knowledge, controls, exacting specifications, close tolerances and measurements are supplementing and often supplanting older practical insights and experience.

The newer technologies, materials, consumer demands and appetites are creating new industries. Older ones are losing out; plants and companies are being liquidated, mergers are pushing out others. The geography of employment is being reshaped. New job concentrations have appeared as older ones have slipped. With these changes have come the problems of developing existing communities to prevent them from becoming ghost towns. The accent on the geographical movement of labour is now greater than ever.

Most significantly the observed rates of change are rising. This places an even greater burden upon individuals. They frequently have to move to new employments, and this calls for great adaptability. More provisions are needed for adjustment and more aids for maintaining personal security and individual competences. The demand for movement has to be met by a willingness to make these moves. People have to recognize their own self-interest in seeking new jobs and fight off resignation and withdrawal. Counselling and support become essential to maintain the less resilient members of society if the goals of universal opportunity are to be attained.

A new work force is developing, shaped by the many post-war demographic, social, and institutional forces. The two wars have left great gaps in the more mature age groups of the population and interfered with the easy continuity of the generations. A high proportion of women are available for employment. Longer periods of education have delayed entrance into the labour market for millions of persons. Advanced education is now shared by greater and greater numbers. Retirement programmes have allowed older persons to withdraw from the labour market.

Enterprises are being established more generally in urban areas. Suburban communities have grown with people demanding the advances, services, and resources of such large societies. Suburbanism has led to some decentralization of jobs away from the core cities, but it has concurrently increased the interrelationships of areas. Metropolitan districts have spread out and engulfed larger areas; the megalopolis has arrived.

The new social goals have penetrated the labour market and created a new industrial society quite unlike any with which we have been acquainted. It is urban in nature; highly changing in character and made up of an essentially optimistic urban type of person restlessly seeking the benefits held out by the new social goals. Opportunities are demanded for constant employment in a society with expanding amenities and services.

The New Role of Government

It is not always easy to define the direction in which we are moving. But some perception of the future is essential if the debate on current issues is not to lose much of its meaning. However, we tend to become bogged down in the details of specific transformations. The functions and operations of government in the labour market are, of course, undergoing vast changes.

To serve the new labour market's needs and the people who are members of it, whether employees or employers, a new policy has been devised—namely, an active manpower policy. It is new in purpose, spirit, and content. Its objective is to assist the economy and society to attain their goals by initiating and implementing programmes rather than by merely being responsive to events and serving people when they seek advice and services. No longer merely a form of mediation, it assures an equal footing to these agencies in decision-making.

Its purpose is to develop a strategy and system of programmes for attaining the full productive employment of the nation's human resources. An active manpower policy seeks to gain this end by harmonizing with its objectives the policies, practices, and services related to the recruitment, training, development, and allocation of manpower by stimulating when appropriate job creation and employment stabilization and by promoting personal security and favourable employee attitudes to economic and technical change and higher productivity.

It covers both public and private enterprises and agencies in the labour market. Necessarily it seeks to gain acceptance by private enterprises of standards and policies which contribute to the realization of public goals and complement the services and aids offered by public agencies. In fact, the enterprise itself is increasingly expected to carry the greater part of the burden of adjustment. Its intimate knowledge of the problems and personnel facilities, personnel expertise and organization cannot be matched. An increasingly close relationship is therefore developing between public and enterprise authorities to create an integrated national manpower programme; a development which surprises its very participants. Private managements are called upon to perform public services and invited to use public facilities or make their own available to public agencies. Governments are employing co-ordination, educational techniques, technical assistance, mutually agreed guidelines, financial and other incentives, and, in the last resort, legislative action to induce and achieve this total programme.

But above all the public manpower agency keeps its goals clearly in mind. By employing persuasion, incentives, and other levers it encourages other governmental agencies and private bodies to conform to these goals, always keeping in mind that through active advice and participation much can be gained. The test of success is not the promulgation of policy, of course, but the degree of effectiveness in reaching the goals. Therefore it constantly monitors developments, tests results, considers alternative action, and offers substitutes when new solutions are appropriate. All agencies in the labour market must therefore work together to find and apply sound and effective policies. In the last analysis the nation demands an active manpower policy.

The New Role of Management

The management of personnel is changing just as general management itself is. A more rational approach is replacing an autocratic and paternalistic one. The emphasis now is upon a stable, productive work-force to be attained by appropriate incentives, benefits, and new co-operative relationships between management and the work-force. Joint consultation and negotiations with the union to bring about changes are replacing unilateral action. Employee participation in decision-taking is often reinforcing joint decision-making. Unions are increasingly being accepted as necessary complementary institutions to management in the operation of the enterprise. The productive utilization of personnel is being viewed as a common purpose and the culmination of joint efforts by both management and the employee.

Personnel development has gained a new high priority in the enterprise. While originally solely an employer-oriented activity limited to management personnel, it is being extended to the lower levels, often under trade-union pressure. No longer is the foreman entrusted with its full responsibility. The central personnel organization is also taking over the responsibility for the production employees, whether blue collar, white collar, or white coverall, as well as management and executive personnel.

Advance planning has become a necessity with the growing demands for manpower and the inability to obtain specifically trained groups in the open labour market. Labour budgeting is being done both for daily operational and long-term needs. It is used both for major and minor innovations. While originally employed for production managers, advance manpower planning is becoming an integral part of general planning, and, in fact, manpower-planners are indispensable adjuncts of all facilities and financial planning.

This widening of his responsibilities has raised the status of the personnel and industrial relations manager and his critical role in the life of the enterprise. In some instances his title has been advanced to that of vice-president to indicate his new executive role. In any event his position has become vital to total policy-making. In Europe the most publicized illustration is the appointment of labour directors in the German coal and steel industry, but comparable developments may be reported, particularly in Great Britain.

The present emphasis is on internal adjustment of personnel to changing demands rather than reliance upon dismissals and displacement. Transfers, training, and attrition are the primary tools of adaptation. While severance pay is employed to pay off some persons, the preference has shifted away from this solution. Labour turnover may be more costly than internal adjustment and may handicap an enterprise in the recruitment of new personnel. More thought is being given to advance planning as a tool for finding ways of solving problems within the enterprise. The result is a contribution to sound industrial relations.

The personnel services have of necessity been extended from mere record-keeping. They have been enlarged to include organizations for training and personnel development. These involve not only the use of internal facilities but also those available in industrial circles and in the community at large. The latter are gaining increasing favour as the economies of such operations are being recognized. Besides personnel planning some have responsibilities for helping to develop organizational structures. The traditional services such as collective bargaining, handling of works councils, remuneration, benefits, recruitment, employee communications, medical services, safety, and security of course continue.

The job environment is a significant determinant of attitudes, and new interest has been shown in this field. This includes not only attention to safety factors but also those affecting health and social attitudes within the plant. The importance of employee groupings has become so well recognized that some are carefully studying work organization from the point of view of appropriate supervision, social relations, and ultimately productivity.

A new sensitivity has also developed towards reactions to industry performance by the public at large and the immediate community. The more frequent promulgation of guides for industrial behaviour by industrial associations, professional groups, or governmental bodies has made it necessary to consider them in relation to local policy formulation and decisions.

Managements have to avoid flaunting public opinion, for the price of indifference is eventually very high. Foreign firms which have closed plants in Europe have produced considerable dissatisfaction and will in future have to find other solutions. Similarly companies must consider the effect of their policies on the community and anticipate them with appropriate programmes.

Companies are increasingly expected to employ voluntarily a cross-section of the labour supply without the need for quotas of secondary or marginal groups to be imposed on them. Finally, it is hoped the management will through special programmes help to achieve social policies such as assisting marginal groups to become more productive members of society.

A new liberal and experimental attitude towards existing techniques and methods is becoming more common. Research and academic reflections and theories are being considered more seriously. Tests which result in biased selection or discriminate against special groups are expected to be revised and improved. Older techniques such as job evaluation and wage incentives which seem to be less useful in our present era are being re-examined, revised, or supplanted by more appropriate ones. Personnel and industrial-relations management is therefore entering a new era and has to be more self-critical and readier to consider new ways.

The New Role of Employees

Some of the major changes in the characteristics of the work-force have already been described. The new attitudes are equally relevant. First there is a greater tolerance towards change and innovation. Having been raised, or at least living, in urban areas and during periods of continuing full employment and rising living standards, the employee is generally aware of the benefits of innovation and the possibilities of sharing in them. Resistance is likely to reflect a bargaining stance rather than a determination to be obstructive. Security and benefits are the objectives. There is a new insistence on professional status, with the right to assistance and support to help the individual develop and advance through his occupational life and adapt to the varying demands made on him.

This view of his economic position is complemented by a second important and growing factor. It is the right to the consideration and settlement of his grievances. Complaints are viewed not only as a method of improving one's personal position, but also as a way of stimulating management's own performance. Complaints uncover the shortcomings in the operations of the enterprise. To be effective in submitting complaints and securing a voice in the economic machine, group identity and cohesion have become important. Former constraints on unionism among non-blue workers are giving way to a recognition of the benefits and ultimately to organization.

The New Role of Trade Unions

The trade union is experiencing considerable difficulty in discerning its new role in modern society. Its past weighs heavily upon it. Its role has been that of standard-bearer of the opposition to highlight discontent and inequities, prescribe long-term solutions or standards, and bargain for short-term advances towards its goals. Its usual stance has been protective rather than innovatory, except when the situation became so desperate that it prescribed radical institutional reforms. Its tradition does not encourage it to sponsor programmes which create risks for its members, as it still finds the protection for them is inadequate, and is in any case constitutionally suspicious of change.

In the field of national and industrial policy it offers counsel and participates in advisory agencies: it is active in the decision-making processes. But it has been reluctant to become a decision-taker. The trade union recognizes this dilemma, for it represents the people who suffer the greater impact, and it cannot easily assume the responsibility for taking the decision which brings about the change.

Many frustrations have been experienced in evolving new strategies. The trade union had counted on the social-security systems to effect social justice and equity in income distribution, and found that this instrument served only to protect the insured from risks, and then often inadequately. The redistribution of income has occurred primarily among the insured.

Participation in the formulation of economic policy has also proved of limited importance. Unless the union could effectively bargain and use its economic strength at the job, plant, or industrial level it could again only advise. The seat of overall economic political power remained far removed from its leverage, usually with the Government and/or the business innovator and investor. Moreover, over-centralization of such power ultimately foreshadowed a curb on its overt influence.

The union has therefore to reconcile its view of the public well-being with that of its own self-interest and freedom of action. It remains protective of its members' interests and in permanent opposition, and accepts the role of counsellor rather than decision-taker.

Relations with members have also changed. Conceived as a lever for the individual to secure him protection through numbers and cohesion, the union is now also expected to assist in the realization of a man's expectations for individual development. In an era of full employment, expansion, and growing opportunities the individual in his new professional outlook needs assistance in reaching beyond his present attainments. If the trade union were to maintain traditional class attitudes it would tend to repress these tendencies. In the past it organized or favoured educational efforts largely to compensate for the shortcomings in the public facilities. But now that it has largely won the battle for educational opportunities it is finding a new role—that of helping individuals to find opportunities for preparing themselves for individual promotion.

Trade unions now play many more roles. They, however, continue to act on behalf of their membership—to search for protection and individual opportunity, for advances with security, equity, and freedom without subservience to repressive central direction, and for responsible powers for representation. The trade union emphasizes maximum local rights. An early advocate of collective action and social planning it now insists on joining them with individual rights for complaint and participation in the decision-making process.

Conclusion

Changes in the social setting are affecting all groups in society. Individual expectations and goals have altered. Labour-market needs are different, and the quality of the labour force has improved. There is a demand for policies, practices, and institutions to be modernized. The Government has become an initiator and guide in realizing society's goals.

Management has therefore had to adapt itself. While the enterprise still has precise functions to perform and cannot subordinate its competitive economic ones, it has to comply with social policies and behaviour patterns. Personnel and industrial relations policy necessarily reflects the emphasis on advance planning personnel development, consultation and bargaining with the work-force and satisfaction of employee expectations. With enterprises becoming more clearly tools of the national purpose, personnel policies and practices have to be harmonized with national programmes and policies. While not public servants, they must serve public ends.

Employees are becoming more insistent on a professional status in industry and the right to a voice in the course of the economy. Trade unions remain the spokesmen of complaints concerning basic social goals, but their area of responsibility for criticism and implementation has broadened. They have more representational functions to perform and need more expertise to discharge them. Critic and adviser, they continue to search for ways of discharging their representational functions at all levels and helping individuals to achieve personal advancement. They stress the pre-eminence of human and social values, always aware of the priorities for economic viability and growth. They favour clearly defined national goals, but wish to preserve local freedoms, and rights for the unions were built upon the demand for the individual's rights for expression and effective participation in society and industry.